The Legitimate History of Lies

The Legitimate History of Lies

A History Textbook from Nazi Germany

Translation and Introduction by
Aleksandr Rainis, MA (Hist)

Introduction © Copyright 2011 Aleksandr Rainis
Printed in the USA and Canada
ISBN: 978-1-257-62856-8

The Legitimate History of Lies

To my Grandmother and Grandfather, who survived two totalitarian regimes.

Acknowledgments

There are many individuals involved in creating a book, both directly and indirectly, and I am afraid I could never thank them all. I would like to mention Dr. Robert Ventresca for his encouragement on this project as well as help with the historiographical aspect of the text. My wife deserves thanks for allowing me the time and peace so necessary to complete my work. Huge thanks to Amanda Wilson for helping me with editing and all the finishing touches that made this project what it is today. Thanks also to Dr. S. Creuzberger for helping me with some difficult German slang. To any who I neglected to mention, I am deeply sorry that I have been so forgetful.

Table of Contents

The Legitimate History of Lies

Introduction

A Short History of Lies

*"History is the only laboratory
we have in which to test
the consequences of thought."
- Etienne Gilson*

To many readers, the translation that follows may seem a mere piece of fantastical Nazi propaganda. It outrages the intellect that German youth were expected to believe such fabrications - lies churned out by Goebbels' propaganda machine for the purpose of brainwashing a generation of young Germans. Historical legends were designed to create in the hearts and minds of youth an absolute allegiance to the nation-state and a feeling that to die as a martyr on the altar of the fatherland was the greatest honor. Indeed the goal of totalitarianism, as opposed to every other tyranny in history, was that it did not aim merely to control man's outer actions, but vied for his innermost soul. Propaganda was at the heart of National Socialist Germany. But one must recognize, that particularly in Germany, we may observe a phenomenon that might be called "a legitimate history of lies." In other words, there was a non-Nazi, highly academic, scientific, and philosophical lineage that primed the German populace for an existence based on pure fantasy. It may be surprising to the reader that in an advanced and civilized nation such as Germany, the extreme and fantastical view of history offered by National Socialism was neither unprecedented nor out of the ordinary in its time and place.

The Nazi movement created historical heroes to legitimize a present and immediate movement. Even the man of the here-and-now was one whose ancestry predestined him to a greatness that was as profoundly historical as it was ideological. The Nazis, in their mission, created myths and legends, saints and martyrs. So few past movements were as historically conscious as Nazism. Hanna Arendt went so far as to argue that the very power of the totalitarian ruler as perceived was based not on his supposed perfection, but instead on his ability to interpret the essentially reliable forces in history, forces that could not be disproved by defeat or ruin.[1]

It is understandable, therefore, the emphasis that National Socialism placed on the teaching of history to Germany's *Jungen* – its youth. Political responsibility and duty were posited on knowledge of history. In *Mein Kampf*, Adolf Hitler blamed virtually all of Germany's political problems after the Great War on improper historical education and offered a new

[1] Hanna Arendt. *The Origins of Totalitarianism.* New York: Schocken Books, 1976, 459.

manifesto concerning the proper historical education of German youth.[2]

The textbook translated here, *Volk und Reich der Deutschen*, is of interest for more than reasons of accessibility and convenience. The series is used in the most noteworthy and recent scholarship on Nazi education. It figures quite extensively in Gilbert Blackburn's 1985 study *Education in the Third* Reich. It also appears in the footnotes of Lisa Pine's 2011 book *Education in Nazi Germany* as well as a wide variety of past and recent academic journal articles on the subject. The textbook series' ubiquity and subsequent volumes and editions may attest to widespread dissemination. Thus, it is evident that the books did not survive merely because they were located in one warehouse in an isolated pocket of Germany. A particular copy of the book that survives in Hofstra University's collection on "Nationalism and Exclusion" is stamped as received at "Metz."[3] The copy in my possession is stamped "Posen." While Metz is situated at the very Western frontier of World War II Germany, Posen lies on the Polish frontier. This is by no means irrefutable evidence that the book was used specifically as frontier educational propaganda at Germany's outlying and

---

[2] Adolf Hitler. Ralph Mannheim (trans.). *Mein Kampf.* New York: Houghton Mifflin Company, 1971, 420-1.
[3] Hofstra's collection can be viewed at:
<http://www.hofstra.edu/Libraries/WestCampus/SpecialCollections/sc_rbam_kroul_guide_rev.cfm>

newly acquired territories in the East and West, but this aim was absolutely vital.

Particular attention to eastern settlement is evident in the subtitle of volume seven of the textbook series: *Von der Deutschen Ostsiedlung bis zu den Anfangen Bismarcks*,[4] but it is quite banal. Less banal was the fact that the only popular translated Nazi textbook to date, commonly known as the *Nazi Primer*, had the original German title of *Vom Deutschen Volk und seinem Lebensraum*.[5] Less banal also were the actions of the Nazi government who, perhaps more than coincidentally, established universities at Germany's frontiers. 1940 saw the establishment of a university at Strasbourg, and in 1941, at Posen itself. According to Hans Schleier in his contribution for the 1999 collaboration *Writing National Histories*, these universities were to be bastions of Germandom, established precisely to project their messages to the East and West.[6]

Thus we have the foundation of a body of evidence suggesting a particular educational interest in Germany's annexed territories, which is neither to be taken lightly nor met with surprise. Documentary evidence from the Nuremberg Trials shows a shocking 270 446 hectares of land seized for resettlement in only

---

[4] *From the German Settlement of the East until the Beginning of Bismarck.*

[5] "The German Volk and their Living Space." Fritz Brennecke. Harwood L. Childs (trans.) *The Nazi Primer: Official Handbook for Schooling the Hitler Youth.* New York: Harper and Brothers Publishers, 1938.

[6] Hans Schleier. "German Historiography under National Socialism: Dreams of a Powerful Nation-State and German Volkstum Come True." Burger, Stephan et all. *Writing National Histories: Western Europe Since 1800.* London: Routeledge, 1999, 186.

four small estate offices of the eastern *Reich* including
Posen (over 6 million hectares had been seized in total
by 1943).[7] The new German settlers would naturally be
the focus of a massive educational effort.

    Volk und Reich der Deutschen's audience is also
important. The title, which states the book's audience as
Oberschulen (Highschool) or *Gymnasien* (Preparatory
School) students gives it a special purpose. At the age of
14-18 years old, important decisions must be made as to
what an adolescent's service to the state will be and
whether he will join the army or attend university (if a
choice is even possible to him). It is likely, then, that
special attention would be paid to this particular age
group in recognition of this important time. In line with
Hitler's educational manifesto, Phys-ed became the
most important subject of instruction. Below followed
Biology, Science, Math, and History (for boys). In the
age group of 14-18, three periods a week were devoted
to History.[8] There is evidence that *Volk und Reich der
Deutschen* was used to buttress eugenic biology, so
likewise historical instruction was often
interdisciplinary.[9]

    Once the Nazis gained power in 1933, dramatic
educational reform began. This was the beginning of the

---

[7] James Joseph Sanchez et all. *Nuremberg War Crimes Trial on CD-ROM*. Seattle:
Aristarchus Knowledge Industries, 1995, IMT 03, 1736.

[8] Gregor Ziemer. *Education for Death: The MaKing of a Nazi.* London: Oxford
University Press, 1941, 157.

[9] Amy Beth Carney. " 'As Blond as Hitler:' Fatherhood and Positive Eugenics in the
Third Reich." (M.A. thesis., Florida State University College of Arts and Sciences,
2005), 40.

"Nazification" of education, a wave of reform that became internationally infamous even prior to World War II. One year before the outbreak of war, Howard L. Childs feverishly translated and published *The Nazi Primer: official handbook for schooling Hitler youth.* During the war, Gregor Ziemer's *Education for Death: The making of a Nazi* enjoyed the status of a best seller. And, in the aftermath of allied victory, the Nuremberg prosecutors referred to educational reform as the key to the bending of German will and the pacification of Nazi enemies.[10]

In the modern industrial age as in the history classes of National Socialist Germany, textbooks offered the uniformity in education essential to a powerful and centralized educational system. But despite the attendant industry of modernity, history textbooks were not available immediately after the 1933 acquisition of power – and old heretical textbooks would certainly not suffice. It would take at the very least three to four years to produce viable textbooks, and in the mean time the Nazis ran crash courses in an ad-hoc manner to "re-educate" teachers.[11] Textbooks were not initially used, but instead teachers were expected to lecture, and lecture material was largely drawn from meetings imbued with SA men reminiscing about their experiences in the trenches of the Great War.[12]

---

[10] Sanchez, IMT 01, 103, 572, IMT 02, 546-7.
[11] Claudia Koonz. *The Nazi Conscience.* Cambridge: The Belknap Press of Harvard University Press, 2003, 137.
[12] Koonz, 138.

Textbooks were not distributed to students even when they were made available, but instead given to teachers. Students could not be permitted to interpret the text themselves and as Gregor Ziemer noted, classes were conducted in lectures, not discussions. The particular book in this study is thus appropriately stamped *"nur für den Unterrichsgebrauch des Lehrers."*[13]

Thus *Volk und Reich der Deutschen, Klasse 1* which was still in its first edition in 1941 (as evidenced by the absence of edition notations present in 1942 editions, and by the existence of 1942 copies in their second edition) represents the coming of age of Nazi textbook production. From 1939 (the earliest date known) to 1943, new updated editions appeared each year, but not in every *Klasse* (Volume).

Revisions to books abounded in a state paranoid of being discredited. It did not take much to make a previously orthodox textbook completely outdated. In fact, the whole series of *Volk und Reich der Deutschen* became instantly outdated and even heretical with one decree from Martin Bormann by order of the *Führer* in 1941.

Before World War II began, the German *Fraktur* font had enjoyed widespread Nazi admiration and use as a truly nationalist, patriotic typeface. Books, street signs, government documents and certificates were widely printed in this font, commonly known as "gothic." Heinrich Himmler was convinced of the

---

[13] "Only for the instructional application of lecturers." Reppich, I.

German nature of the typeface, and held some credibility as the founder of the historical-biological studying circle called the *Ahnenerbe*, (which later became associated with medical experiments at the war-crimes trials). A defence council member at Nuremberg noted that Himmler was committed to the close cultural heritage of the Indo-Germanic peoples, so much so he alleged far reaching ties between Japanese characters and gothic script. This of course had invaluable propaganda purposes anticipating the formal Japanese alliance.[14]

The rather abrupt and revolutionary "discovery" by Bormann that outdated the textbooks is perhaps most simply expressed in a letter by a critic who wrote with antagonistic irony "[…] *die deutsche Schrift sei nicht deutsche* […]"[15] Historical research had supposedly uncovered the Jewishness of the gothic script used by German publishers. In his memorandum, Bormann wrote that historically the Jews owned the first printing presses, for which they designed the *Fraktur* font, now called "Schwabacher Jewish-Letters." Gothic font had been banned by Hitler after 1941, and the Roman typeface was to be substituted at every level of bureaucracy. It is especially of interest to note that Bormann's memorandum, while very concise, specifically mentioned that school textbooks were the highest priority for conversion to the new font, while

---

[14] Sanchez, NMT 05, 3207.
[15] "[…] the German script is not German […]" Sanchez, IMT 41, 1025.

other areas of government would undergo a more gradual transition.[16]

While the 1941 copy of *Volk und Reich der Deutschen, Klasse 1* was printed too early to allow for conversion to the new font, the 1942 *Klasse 2* was also printed in the heretical *Fraktur* script. The staggering task of changing the typeset of every book printed in Germany was nearly impossible and is thus revealed (and naturally became more so after the war turned against Germany). Hofstra University's copies of the series date from 1943, two years after the decree. After that year, the typeset might have never been converted at all as the war wound down and resources dwindled.

Other physical qualities of the textbook can also give much insight into the series' usage and production. *Volk und Reich der Deutschen* is an illustrated history with reproductions of hand-drawn sketches by Henry Pauser. The sketches depict historical events and figures within the text. Not only are there nineteen sketches, but also there are sixteen photographs in black and white peppered throughout the 143 pages of text as well. The photographs are very large, and most had to be inserted sideways to fit the 23cm x 16cm (9"x 6 ½")

---

[16] M. Bormann in a circular letter, 3 January 1941. "Letter: Bormann's Schrifterlass – English." n. d., < http://german.about.com/library/gallery/blfoto_fraktur06E.htm> (3 January 2006).

book, perhaps to facilitate the lecturer showing the pictures from the front of the classroom. Hitler appears in three of the sixteen photographs, and needless to say this means more photos are devoted to Hitler than any other one event or figure.

The importance of pictures should not be played down. It is not only the content of the pictures themselves that is important, but the historiographical role illustrations play. Textbooks in Nazi Germany stressed visual "experiences." The reader was encouraged to experience part of history in more than just an intellectual way; illustrations were important to bypass the intellect, to "unlock the soul" from the mind.[17] As 19th Century German historian Henry von Treitschke argued, we must actively, not passively engage in history.[18] Leopold von Ranke, a German historian often misinterpreted as the father of a scientific historical method, once said that history is never science without art.[19]

These pre-Nazi views on the practice of history raise important questions. While historiography was an essential part of the Faculty of History's *Gleichaltung*, its "bringing into line" with Nazi ideology, how different was this historiography from in pre-Nazi times? Historian Stephan Berger argues that little can be said to

---

[17] Koonz, 152.

[18] Henry von Treitschke. Eden and Cedar Paul (trans.) *History of Germany in the Nineteenth Century*. Vol. 5. New York: Ams Press, 1968, 508.

[19] Leopold von Ranke. George G. Iggers, Konrad von Moltke (eds.), William A. Iggers (trans.). *The Theory and Practice of History*. New York: The Bobbs-Merril Co., 1973, 34.

be "genuine Nazi historiography,"[20] but he refers to academia. If anything could assuredly be classified as an official historical view, it would be the made-to-order Nazi textbooks produced and controlled by government directives. While the textbooks were written by academics working with government officials including SS leaders,[21] there was little concern for accuracy or tireless research to falsify theory.[22] And although Walter Frank's call for an official Nazi historiography was unheeded in higher learning[23], the total control exacted on the primary and secondary school system allowed for the development of what one might justifiably argue to be an "official" historical philosophy.

That said, it has become evident in many studies that academic freedom, specifically in History, was hardly impinged upon under Nazism. In his 1968 book, *The German Conception of History*, George Iggers argued that under Hitler, historians were not free, and that many of them found it hard to cope with Nazism.[24] However, two newer studies differ in their findings. Stephan Berger's concern with the lack of true Nazi history partly results from his finding that historians

---

[20] Berger, 38.

[21] Dr. Walter Hohmann et all. *Volk und Reich Der Deutschen, Geschichtsbuch für Oberschulen und Gymnasien, Klasse 2: Indogermanen und Germanen.* 4th ed. Frankfurt am Main: Verlag Otto Salle, 1942, II.

[22] Schleier, 178.

[23] Berger, 38.

[24] George G. Iggers. *The German Conception of History: The National Tradition of Historical Thought from Herder to the Present.* Middletown: Weslegan University Press, 1983, XV, 3.

did retain their autonomy, and that the differences between historians and official ideology were not great enough to be antagonizing.[25] Hans Schleier echoes Berger's findings: historians freely supported and legitimized the regime without much coercion. In fact, the history produced under free scholarship often propagandized better than the Nazi regime did.[26]

To set up a conflict between official historiography and free academia as such might be a false dichotomy. To say that, in true Orwellian fashion, freedom is the ability to say "two and two make four," seems a poor analogy in a culture where, as in Dostoyevsky, the formula "two and two make five" is so attractive. Certainly, a contradiction to official history might bring a threat to inform the Gestapo, especially in cases that involved the new territories and racial unity,[27] but it is evident that in most cases, opposition was simply lacking. We may then assume that the degree to which control was exacted, or whether or not control was exacted at all, what was written in history under Nazism was bound to be amicable to official ideology. A history textbook merely epitomized that ideology by the higher degree of active government involvement.

Volk und Reich der Deutschen, Klasse 1 is, above all, a story of the prime movers in history. The subtitle states that it is a tale of the leaders and heroes of

---

[25] Berger, 38.

[26] Schleier, 184.

[27] Frederick Percyval Reck-Melleczewen. Paul Reubens (trans.). *Diary of a Man in Despair.* London: The Macmillan Company, 1970, 86.

German history, and naturally it is entirely personality-based. There are no events in the table of contents not subordinated to personalities. This may not be characteristic of all Nazi school history textbooks. For example, *Klasse 2* of the series is separated by periods. However, since it deals with a period roughly from the ice age to 1000 AD, this may simply not have been practical. Timetables in this same book are still personality-based, not epoch-based, and even though the book concludes at 1000 AD, Hitler still appears at the top of the chart.[28]

Thus, acknowledging small exceptions of questionable significance, *Volk und Reich der Deutschen* shares in the historiographical tradition discussed in Berger's work *The Search for Normality*. This tradition, especially in Germany, saw history as being made by the hero and the "great man" of history, and was a salient preoccupation of pre-Nazi historiography.[29] The historiography of the book ignores abstractions, while focusing on specific people. George Iggers refers to Dilthey, the 19th Century German Romanticist, when he writes that since thought must be concrete, not abstract, philosophy's mission must be to find an inner-relatedness not in the world, not in natural law, but in men themselves.[30] Claudia Koonz's study concurs,

---

[28] Hohmann, 2.
[29] Berger, 38.
[30] Iggers, 141.

seeing no difference between the "great men" vocation of Nazi textbooks and pre-Nazi textbooks.[31]

But *Volk und Reich der Deutschen, Klasse 1,* is an exception to Koonz's assertion that history lessons "[…] celebrated not Nazi martyrs, but the same generals, rulers, and writers as in pre-Nazi textbooks."[32] While it is true for the most part, an influential historical figure such as Bismarck is given one chapter of the book, while three chapters are devoted to Nazis, one being Hitler, and the other two the comparatively insignificant Herbert Norkus and the Nazi martyr, Horst Wessel. By far the longest chapter of the book, notably, is devoted to Adolf Hitler, who at the time, was not a historical figure at all. In fact, *Volk und Reich der Deutschen* abandons past-tense verbs by the end of the chapter.

What naturally followed educational reform was the adaptation of the pedagogical structure of a History class. Gregor Zeimer notes: "A History class, for instance, should be so organized that it can deviate at any moment from routine and avail itself of new material provided by Nazi activity."[33] Chronology in history was reversed. *Volk und Reich der Deutschen* does not begin with the earliest period; it does not begin with Arminius in 9 AD. The book begins with Hitler and goes back in time from there. The immediate nature of Nazi history is perhaps best exemplified by a history textbook studied in 1934 by Ernest Barker, *Aufbruch der*

---

[31] Koonz, 157.

[32] Ibid.

[33] Zeimer, 17.

Nation, which covers the period from 1914-1933 (only a year previous to its composition!)[34] History, in a traditional sense, was not a subject concerning the past.

The argument might follow that the immediacy of Nazi history as epitomized by the worship of non-historical (Nazi) figures and the fanatical focus on Versailles is perhaps the best demarcation of true National Socialist History from past traditions. This argument, however, is impotent in the context of a historiographical tradition that increasingly viewed the past as immediate (dating back to the development of the first historical journals in Germany).[35] Ranke's rejection of progress and resulting faith in the goodness of man in the present was epitomized by the quip that "every epoch is immediate to God."[36] Philosophical truth, according to this tradition, was not to be gleaned from man's senses and rationality, but from history - an imaginative and intuitive exploration of the human experience. This tradition became increasingly radicalized during and after the Great War. The consequence was, as Modris Eksteins writes in his study of World War I and modernity, that "[h]istory was, in short, more a matter of the present than of the past and of intuition rather than rational analysis."[37]

---

[34] Ernest Barker. *A Nazi School History Textbook*. No. 11. Westminster: "Friends of Europe" Publications, 1934, 5.

[35] Gabriel Ricci. *Time Consciousness: The Philosophical Uses of History*. New Brunswick: Transaction Publishers, 2002, 35.

[36] Ranke, 53.

[37] Modris Eksteins. *Rites of Spring: The Great War and the Birth of the Modern Age*. Toronto: Lester and Orpen Dennys Ltd., 1989, 194.

History, to frame the issue in theological terms, was the Revelation of universal and timeless Truth. The idea was not a Nazi machination, but the legacy of German philosophers like Kant, Hegel, and Johann Herder who reacted against the rationalism of the Enlightenment. Henry von Treitschke praised Goethe when he wrote "[...] the poet gives a comprehensible existence of heaven through his boldly sketched figures of sacred history [...]"[38] The inevitable praise of success was a logical consequence of the theory of Revelation. 19th Century German historians of this tradition, such as Leopold von Ranke, could not conceive of any historical event where the higher moral energy had not belonged to the victor.[39] Ranke wondered: "How could anything be without the divine basis of its existence?"[40] In fact, one of Treitschke's prime criticisms of Ranke was that he failed to emphasize the moral superiority that explained the victory of Protestantism.[41]

Thus it is understandable why historians supported Hitler after his success in pre-war Germany and after successful expansion in the East before Stalingrad. In the field of History, might made right. Since history was the key to truth and values in the present, might is eternally right. To paraphrase Adolf Hitler, history proves that one who possesses no might

---

[38] Treitschke, 506.
[39] Iggers, 82.
[40] Ranke, 38.
[41] Treitschke, 572.

has no use for right.[42] Thus historian Hans Schleier sees, with ample justification, that historiography after 1933 was a revival of old traditions, not a fabrication of new ones.[43]

Goethe's sacred history remained sacred for the Nazis. As *Aufbruch der Nation* argues, the spirit of the soldiers of the Great War was continually undermined from outside and within from those enemies who wanted to distract Germans from the "holiness" of the war.[44] Indeed, volumes could be written on the religiosity of the German historical tradition and the revelation in disguise that the Nazis represented, but this is not the goal of this guide to the translation.

The chapter of *Volk und Reich der Deutschen* devoted to Adolf Hitler is the tale of a messianic Christ figure who wanders the land and performs miracles. He saves his field commander's life in the Great War, captures countless Frenchmen by himself, and fights for Germany's rebirth. He creates relics by his holy touch that laymen long for, gives a poor war-invalid a job, turns the other cheek for a former Communist, ironically admires the spirit of a young crippled *Pimpf*, gives a poor worker his raincoat, and leads Germany on a glorious string of military victories. And like Jesus expelling the moneychangers from a holy place, Hitler frees Germany from the control of the Jewish race, a race that before Hitler, according to the textbook, "*[…]*

---

[42] Sanchez, IMT 02, 547.
[43] Schleier, 177.
[44] Barker, 7.

führten in den Zeitungen und im Reichstag das große Wort."[45]

It is clear from the book the prophetic nature of the Nazi movement in a Divine Plan. Hitler sleepwalks in the direction that Providence dictates. The textbook asserted that although Hitler wanted to be an architect, God himself had planned for Hitler to become an entirely different kind of builder.[46] In another section the book asserted the Nazi movement was one in which a man sacrificed his blood on the *"Altar des Vaterlandes."* – on the "Altar of the Fatherland".[47] And the Blood Flag, it argued, is the *"heiligstes"* – the "holiest" symbol of the movement on which the *"Märtnrer"* – "Martyrs" spilled their blood for "German Freedom."[48] Another textbook, as Gregor Zeimer reported (a biography of the *Führer*), referred to Hitler as a figure with a halo, a soldier who possessed a saint's soul, and a true leader with the "kiss of God on his brow."[49] In Vivian Oglivie's 1933 study on education under Hitler, she noted:

> Children themselves told me that the teacher had said in the religion lesson that Hitler was the second Jesus, but greater than the first, because he had not only one Power but the whole world against him. They were also told that he once

---

[45] "[…] did all the talKing in the newspapers and parliament." Reppich, 8

[46] Reppich, 3.

[47] Reppich, 9.

[48] Ibid.

[49] Zeimer, 112.

nearly lost his sight and it was miraculously restored.[50]

Adolf Hitler had replaced Christ as a messiah and a prophet; and as a Prussian *Junker* noted, the youth of a once pious culture even tore crucifixes from walls and cast them to the street with the words "Lie there, you dirty Jew!"[51]

Volk und Reich der Deutschen shares in the German historiographical tradition of seeing in history God's plan. This was often the only force that saved historians of previous eras, like Ranke and Humboldt, from complete philosophical relativism (as a consequence of their rejection of natural law).[52] The conceit of the Nazis historical vision is thus not a unique trait of the history of the 1933-45 era, but rather the continuity of a historiographical tradition deeply rooted in German history.

Nazi history would deviate from the archetypal Rankean tradition in German historiography markedly, however. Ranke was renowned for his arduous labor to show history *wie es eigentlich gewesen* - how it actually was. Ranke, for his pure love of truth, relied on *sources*.

By contrast, the first generations of Nazi textbooks, according to Claudia Koonz, quoted solely from Hitler. In *Volk und Reich der Deutschen*, virtually the

---

[50] Vivian Oglivie. *Education under Hitler*. No. 17. Westminster: "Friends of Europe" Publications, 1934, 6.

[51] Reck-Melleczewen, 22.

[52] Iggers, 111.

only source material acknowledged is *Mein Kampf*. The rest of the book contains little reference to any source material, and relates poetically written tales with information that is inherently non-verifiable, comparable to some popular, non-academic histories and autobiographies, but hardly appropriate for a preparatory school in an advanced country. The warning was explicit in Gregor Zeimer's reading of a manual for teachers: do not produce intellectuals. No individual is to be more brilliant than another is. Too much knowledge paralyzes the will.[53]

There is certainly no doubt education was the product of government policy. As mentioned earlier, Hitler had a specific manifesto for the historical education of the German youth. Hitler wished to impart upon the youth a real national enthusiasm, a historical vision based on the accomplishment of great men:

> They [the former educators] did not understand how to make the really significant men of our people appear as outstanding heroes in the eyes of the present, to concentrate the general attention upon them and thus create a unified mood. They were not able to raise what was glorious for the nation in the various subjects of instruction above the level of objective presentation [...][54]

---

[53] Zeimer, 19-21.
[54] Hitler, 424.

Hitler continued, railing against History as the mere acquisition of knowledge, proclaiming that:

> [n]o one seemed to consider it possible that some day there might come a war that would thoroughly test the inner steadfastness of our patriotic convictions in drumfire and clouds of gas. But when it came, the absence of the highest national passion brought the most frightful consequences.[55]

Compare Hitler's argument with the nineteenth century, in Ranke:

> France had only attained her supremacy because, in the midst of her turbulence, she had known how to keep the feeling of national unity more alive, and how to strain her national resources in an extraordinary expansion for the single purpose of war.[56]

And compare this vision also with the unabashed pinnacle of pre-Nazi nationalist History. In von Treitschke's 1879 *History of Germany in the Nineteenth Century*, one finds a passage that anticipates Hitler's

---

[55] Hitler, 425.
[56] Ranke, 97.

own utterances. In praise of the historian Frederick Dahlman, Treitschke writes:

> Throughout there was displayed a clear recognition of the freedom of historical greatness, of the nobility of our classical culture, of those pious emotional energies which combine to maintain the state – an elevated outlook which had nothing in common with the arrogance of the Enlightenment.[57]

Hitler's "highest national passions" and Treitschke's "pious emotional energies" served the same goal. In fact, Treitschke expresses precisely the same notions in marginally different language. There is a deep approval of the *moral* freedom of the historical genius, the worship of nationalism, and the hatred of objectivity. Treitschke criticized the German historical compilation the *Staatslexikon* precisely because it "sang in all cases the old song" of French reason.[58] This is the effrontery Treitschke speaks of. The pretension to objective knowledge and natural law, the handmaiden of the Enlightenment, was abstract and "arrogant". In the same way, the historian Johann Droysen asserted that subjectivity was preferable to objectivity because of its purposefulness instead of its capability to produce "sterile generalizations."[59] What the mass movement

---

[57] Treitschke, 575.
[58] Treitschke, 573.
[59] Iggers, 112.

needed, according to Hitler, was "[…] not objectivity (read weakness), but will and power."[60]

We cannot, then, refer to *Volk und Reich der Deutschen's* bias or personality worship as genuinely Nazi phenomena. Even 1914 saw the worship of the very same figures featured in the 1939 *Volk und Reich der Deutschen* with the exception of the Nazi martyrs.[61] One notable example of pre-Nazi historical fabrication was the Battle of Tannenberg. The famous German victory of World War I actually took place in Allenstein, but in the interest of Pan-German nationalism, it was dubbed the Battle of Tannenberg to efface the defeat of German Knights there in 1410. Racist tendencies such as anti-Semitism had also been acceptable in historical writings since Treitschke. But while previous historical philosophy merely played down the importance of empiricism and facts, Nazi history absolutely despised them.[62] *Volk und Reich der Deutschen* seems to conform to that assertion when it brazenly claims that Hitler founded the NSDAP, while he technically only changed its name.[63] In the textbook version of the Nazi march on the *Feldherrnhalle*, Ludendorf's fantastical march through the lines of dumbfounded German police (while Hitler is escaping) is entirely omitted from an otherwise fantastical book.[64] The textbook makes

---

[60] Hitler, 338.
[61] Eksteins, 195.
[62] Schleier, 178.
[63] Reppich, 6.
[64] Reppich, 9.

simple, isolated, one-sentence claims such as the loss of the Great War was clearly the result of *"Verräter und Juden"* – "Traitors and Jews."[65] World War II begins with a French and Polish attack on Germany.[66] This is only the first chapter of the book.

Vivian Oglivie's study shows that what the Nazis did not lie about, they alluded to by omission. In the Roman's contact with German tribes, Oglivie notes, "[t]he impression was given that the Romans made first contact with civilisation when they met these tribes."[67]

Hans Schleier notes that there is indeed a lineage of anti-objectivity in German historiography[68], but Nazis did not only subjectively select their facts, they fabricated them or mired them in deceiving and misleading language. Oglivie notes in her study that the changing of cultural history was such that new Nazi verses were added to old German songs.[69] There is a difference between subjectivity as presenting merely a part of reality, and fabrication, the creating of an unreal reality. This frightening truth, one where even past songs are modified so that their historical existence is bound up with the party, is where George Orwell drew his inspiration for the mutability of history:

---

[65] Reppich, 6.
[66] Reppich, 15.
[67] Oglivie, 11.
[68] Schleier, 178.
[69] Oglivie, 12.

> In his own schooldays, Winston remembered, in
> the late 'fifties, it was only the helicopter that the
> Party claimed to have invented; a dozen years
> later, when Julia was at school, it was already
> claiming the aeroplane; one generation more,
> and it would be claiming the steam engine.[70]

This is where *Volk und Reich der Deutschen*
seemingly breaks free of the stream of continuity in
German historiography, without breaking its tether.

It is truly a departure from the fidelity of Ranke,
but the path from subjectivity to fabrication was an
especially short one in the context of culturally
acceptable historical philosophy in Germany. The most
successful legacies were left by historians who, when
confronted with reason or intuition, would quickly
choose the latter. Just as morality (and reality) was not
the same for everyone, Treitschke noted, neither was
the past. It was wrong to judge historical figures to the
standard of a "private morality."[71] Treitschke thus noted
that universal history was a devious path, and that the
German fairytale writer Jacob Grimm did not preserve
mere art with his pen, but guarded the treasures of a
primal age "as a priest guards a sacred relic."[72] The
misunderstanding was that, as a commentary on a Nazi

---

[70] George Orwell. *Animal Farm – Nineteen Eighty-Four.* London: Guild Publishing, 1978, 210.
[71] Treitschke, 578.
[72] Treitschke, 582.

school history textbook exemplifies, "[…] that in a great country, which has done so much for the scientific study of history (read here, Ranke), the writing of history should fall to the level of legend."[73]

Although admittedly, the overall conclusions one can draw from the instance of a single history textbook in Nazi Germany are not dramatic or sweeping, *Volk und Reich der Deutschen* is especially illustrative of themes historians have dealt with perennially. There are both totalitarian issues detailed and allusions to universal recurring problems in the historical profession. There are details of mass education in the modern state and the wresting of the transcendental from the church to the benefit of the state. Perhaps in the end this study will provide more questions than answers.

Nonetheless, it is clear that Nazi historiography was a radicalization of previous trends in German historical philosophy. National Socialism brought this philosophy to its logical end, and as such, pushed German philosophy forward. The era following the Great War was not a period of change in German philosophy, but rather as Modris Eksteins argues "[…] the radicalism in Germany, rather than being subdued, was accentuated."[74] Nazi history was thus an avant-garde art form that did not throw out tradition, but

---

[73] Barker, 3.

[74] Eksteins, xvi.

radicalized it. It was, artistically, a neoclassicist movement.

The absurd logic of totalitarianism was that if something was not true, the ruling clique would make it so. Hanna Arendt argues that "[w]hat convinces masses are not facts, and not even invented facts, but only the consistency of the system which they are presumably part."[75] The belief in immutable laws of history, Arendt says, is the device by which totalitarian governments base their infallibility and prophesize their own actions. Defeats are thus only temporary, because history is bound to assert itself in the long run. Historians, perhaps more than other professionals, had been unwittingly blazing a path for totalitarianism.[76]

If we deal with the question of whether Nazi history textbooks were entirely different from the stream of previous German history writing, we should also ask how different Nazi history textbooks were from the histories of any other country in the era of nations and nationalism. As Ernest Barker, professor of Political Science at Cambridge University noted in his preface to analyzing a Nazi history textbook, every nation has its legends that it creates about itself, and it expresses those legends in popular history books and story books. Barker asserted that they are good so far as they instill a sensible national pride, bad if they foster prejudice.[77] It

---

[75] Arendt, 460.

[76] George Iggers shies away from the strength of this statement, but stated that historians contributed to the rise of authoritarianism. See: Iggers, xv.

[77] Barker, 2.

is true that other nations wrote spiteful histories that depicted their enemies as tyrants and skewed historical vision in their favor, but can we regard some nation's legends as good and others bad? Although we might meet Nazi legends with a feeling of repulsion, evil, and even disbelief, can we say they are wrong while holding our own to be patriotic or at least harmlessly benign?

The moral difference between pride and prejudice, in matters of nation, is insignificant. National pride is a sense of unearned pride that one receives merely by the chance of being born to a particular national group – it is the reverse of national guilt and it is equally as unjust for an individual to be praised or condemned for his nationality. National prejudice is simply the world-view of someone who accepts the philosophical validity of unearned "national" pride (or guilt). It assumes that every other individual in the world must be judged on the basis of his chance birth into a particular nationality, and not on his personal character. Barker argues that it is the *degree* of unearned pride that can be bad; he expects his readers to accept that a little evil and effrontery to justice is good, a lot is bad.

There is a certain difference, however, between the kind of nationalism *Volk und Reich der Deutschen* expresses and more traditional forms. Hanna Arendt argues that more common national chauvinism references the actual past of a nation, while the innovative totalitarian concept, tribal nationalism, "[…]

dares to measure a people, past and present, by the yardstick of exalted inner qualities and inevitably rejects its visible existence, tradition, institutions, and culture."[78] Tribal nationalism in Germany rejected all German realities; it evaluated men by their "German soul" belonging to every member no matter where they lived.

Volk und Reich der Deutschen either makes an outrageous claim based on this philosophy or accurately reflects a population committed to it. As Hitler is annexing territory in the early war, Germans outside the *Reich*, using the familiar form of "you," are calling out to Hitler, and begin to ask: *"Führer, wann holst du uns heim ins Reich?"*[79] Each German is "home" in the *Reich*; it is a spiritual home that does not pay regard to history, culture, or geographical distance.

Every historical figure covered in the book is transformed from a being of genuine existence to the protagonist of a moral parable. They embody supremely the moral and physical qualities of the German and his soul; they are artifacts of the Nazi doctrine. Hindenburg gives bread to a poor classmate, Schlageter wins a snowball fight as a child, Bismarck saves a drowning horseman, Queen Luise, as a child, saves another child from a storm and brings her into a castle. These are not events of any historical significance, and it could be argued that they are

---

[78] Arendt, 293.

[79] *Führer*, when will you bring us home into the *Reich*? Reppich, 15.

unverifiable, but they serve to demonstrate the supposed moral qualities inherent in every German, regardless of their geographic location, chronology, or even their own consciousness. These heroes are Germans and only Germans are heroes.

In terms of historiography and culture, Germany merely exemplified the extreme and most advanced form of nationalism. Just as Germany had been the most advanced nation in arts and science, a nation of *Dichter und Denker*, the poet and the philosopher, so was it a place where the most modern art forms thrived.

But all peoples wrote nationalist histories. Mystical legends and martyrs were created by all modern nation-states. Indeed, historians must come to terms with the fact that historical study itself finds its origin in Greek poetry. However, most poignant in all of this talk of comparing nationalist histories is the philosophical susceptibility of the historian. How does he criticize Nazi historiography apart from other nationalist histories from a historian's perspective while not rejecting the concept of unearned guilt from the perspective of a philosopher? Peter Novick notes that "[…][v]ery few historians have any philosophical training, or even inclination. (Not a crime; not even blameworthy; most philosophers are rotten historians.)"[80] There is a logical hierarchy ignored here. Philosophers need not be historians to practice.

---

[80] Peter Novick. *That Noble Dream: The "Objectivity Question" and the American Historical Profession.* New York, Cambridge University Press, 1988, 11.

Historians, or any other researcher, can not select their subjects of study without a conscious or unconscious code of values. Historians must be philosophers before they are historians. In order to practice their noble profession, a historian must consider ethics, and all are asked to do this in their professional conduct. How can one do this without ethical thinking? Moreover, how can one truly identify the fallacy of nationalist history without knowing the fallacies of the ideas themselves?

The translation that follows must not be viewed as a mere piece of propaganda appearing as an unprecedented aberration in history with no lineage. The imaginative stories, fantastical encounters, and simplistic ideological claims were not devices invented *ex nihilo* by the radicals of the National Socialist movement. These devices had a legitimate history in what many would claim to be the misguided fantasies of German Romanticism. German historiography cared more about the hearts of men than their minds. The more I consider the origins of totalitarianism, the more I am convinced that it was the preceding generations of scientists, philosophers, and artists who made totalitarianism possible. Without technology, knowledge, and the mechanistic model of existence provided by science, without a revolution in ethics, and without a means of promulgating new ideas, totalitarianism could not have existed. Outside of actually living in 19th and early 20th century Germany, it is hard to understand the mindset of a people subject to the ideas of these oracles of national culture. The ways that German theorists, in the era before and during National Socialism, claimed students must experience history may seem alien to us, but as the proverb goes, "the past is a foreign country."

A. Rainis, 2011.

Translator's Note

This project has been one several years in the making. Five years ago I began this translation as a project at King's University College when I noticed that there was little available to English readers in the way of original Nazi educational publications. I hope this translation will be an aid to educational researchers, historians, and casual readers with an interest in discovering what students in German high-school classes actually learned during the National Socialist period. This book marks the first time a translation of a Nazi history textbook has been published since the 1930s, and is the only such project currently in print.

The German *Fraktur* font , in which the original textbook was typeset, is very difficult for the English eye to read, and this feature held its own learning curve, but generally my method has two steps. The first is to translate the text into a rather literal word-for-word translation, awkward but grammatically correct, and the second is to make the text more natural to the English reader. In doing this I have tried to retain the original meaning of the text as much as possible, but there are always words and concepts which simply have no English equivalent and must be interpreted by the translator and related in the best way to the reader. I have extensively annotated the text to convey to the reader these problems and shortcomings, as well as to provide historical insights into some of the textbook's claims.

I have kept many of the place names and many common German words (sometimes, but not always *Volk, Reich*) etc in the original German. Certain place names, where the English reader might not understand the text otherwise, have been translated (Munich for example). It is always a challenge to decide whether to change the names of the historical figures themselves (Heinrich to Henry etc.) and there is no hard and fast rule, so one must use his discretion, as I did.

I have also, from time to time, asked for the help of native German speakers to help translate a particular sentence or passage. At times it seems that no amount of academic study can provide one with the tools to understand subtleties such as slang, dialects, and word usages that have their own propaganda purposes to which we might otherwise be blind. I have included notes were possible to share with the reader these subtleties so they do not go unnoticed.

Finally, there are some sub-chapters from the original textbook that for reasons of time and interest did not make it into my translation. I apologize for this shortcoming but I still felt the material I could make available was worth seeing in print.

The Legitimate History of Lies

1: A Scan of the Original 1941 Cover

The Volk and Reich of the Germans

History Book for High-school and Gymnasium

Volume 1

Of Leaders and Heroes

Stories
out of German History

by

Dr. Hans Reppich

1941

Published by Otto Salle in Frankfurt am Main

The *Führer*

Adolf Hitler Studies History

On the 20th of April 1889 Adolf Hitler was born in the old German city of Braunau am Inn. His father, the son of a poor farmer, had worked through his assiduity and ability to a career as a customs officer. His mother had also descended from farmers. Both father and mother wished that their son should become a great civil servant. Therefore they sent him to higher education in Linz.

There, Adolf Hitler was able to study. His favorite subjects were History, Geography, and Visual Art. Of the history of the German people he could not hear enough.

As he was alone one day at home, he searched in a bookcase of his fathers for something to read. There he found two volumes with many illustrations. It was the history of the war between France and Germany 1870/71. He began to read and view the illustrations. Still further he read; he could not take in enough. His father permitted him to keep the books until he read them entirely. He sat day after day with burning cheeks and blazing eyes and read and read. Aye, the Germans, they were real men![81] Over and over again they had defeated the French. And at the battle of Sedan they

---

[81] *Ja, die Deutschen, das waren Kerle.*

captured Napoleon with their great army. And at last Bismarck founded the greater German *Reich*. In Versailles at Paris they had a great celebration in the palace, and the old King Wilhelm was there to be proclaimed the *Kaiser* of the Germans.

There was one thing he could not apprehend. In the book, there was nothing mentioned that the Austrians had also battled along with Germany. This hurt him. How was that so? They were, after all, also German. Again, he found more sadness. The Germans in the Reich, they could be elated. They had a brave army and a strong Reich. Virtually all of the German people were there. They speak the German language. In his land, in Austria-Hungary, there were all kinds. 52 million persons lived there. Only 12 million were German. The other 40 million were Czech, Polish, Hungarian, Serbian, Rumanian, and others. In Austria one could not be proud as a German. The Germans were the best soldiers, the most faithful civil servants, and the most industrious workers. About them nothing could be said. The others were dominant.

How Adolf Hitler wished to become an Architect

Adolf Hitler was but thirteen years old when his father died. And only a few years afterwards, death also took his mother. But Adolf Hitler did not lose his audacity. What his father had done in his past, he would also attempt: to help himself through life alone.

He packed his bag, along with his things his drawings and all of his money – fifty florins. Rife with hope, he set out to Vienna. There he aimed to gain acceptance to art school, in the academy, and submit his drawings. A professor with a large pair of spectacles looked them over, then looked at Hitler and said:

"Is that all?"Hitler replied in the affirmative. He had to hear this now:

"You wish to become a painter? That will not do. For that you have no gift. But you can become a master builder, an architect. That one can see from your drawings. Apply to the school of architecture."

That was crushing. So long had he struggled toward his goal, to be a painter. And now it was all in vain. But one hope still remained. Quickly, to the school of architecture! Again a professor looked through his drawings and asked him where he had gone to school. The professor could not believe that Adolf Hitler had not attended a building design school. So good were his drawings.

But he who wishes to attend an architectural school must first have worked through a high school in the final grade. That Adolf Hitler could not do. He became ill and had to drop out. When the instructor heard this, he rejected him. All of his hopes were sunk.

What should he do now? For a while he lived on his money, but it would not be enough for long. Then came adversity, and he had to find work or go hungry. He inquired about work in a construction company.

"We will employ only an experienced worker", said the manager.

"I am just as able as the experienced workers," answered Hitler.

From that, came rejection: "That won't do."

Already Hitler was at the door and leaving when the manager said this:

"We will try it this once."

So Adolf Hitler became a supplementary construction worker. He had now to do the most menial tasks: mixing concrete, making mortar, hauling rock. But he was happy because he had work. And in his heart there was still a hope: perhaps he could still become an architect. God's design for him was to be an entirely different kind of architect. Of that he knew not, and no man in the wide world anticipated it.

Dead tired, he came home each evening. He had no remaining strength do devote to learning. Besides, he did not have enough peace there in his room that he had to share with a friend. For him it was too expensive to be alone, he earned too little. His flat was situated in a district of Vienna where only poor people live. In small, confined flats the families with their many children were crowded together. There he learnt of poverty and misery. It was worst for them, those without work and income. Adolf Hitler knew this adversity also, as sometimes he felt it himself. Of that he is still mindful, that each person in Germany find work.

In this time Hitler also became an enemy of the Jews. They lied to the workers in rallies and in the newspapers and cast them off. They were to blame, that the worker hated his fellow comrades. Adolf Hitler perceived how they corrupted his people, and fought keen against them ever since.

He could no longer make a living as a construction worker. He had to earn his bread in another way. And that way arrived. He painted small pictures and sold them. He did not get much for them. He had to live so sparsely and even sometimes go hungry; but he could provide for himself on his own. Now he also had much time to learn. That he did with great industry, day after day. He would constantly procure new books and study for himself. So he gained a vast knowledge.

How Adolf Hitler saved his Field Commander's Life

It was the great World War. Adolf Hitler had enlisted at the beginning of war as a volunteer in the Bavarian regiment. As it happened the Regiment was positioned in France in a difficult struggle.

Attention – march, march! – The List regiment stormed against the enemy. With deadly fire the brave men were decimated and mowed down row after row. The assault came to a halt on enemy positions. It was impossible to go even one step further. The Regiment Commander Lieutenant Colonel Engelhardt was

positioned on the forest edge and searched with
binoculars the best inroad to the enemy. The French had
already detected him! Rattling machinegun fire beat
down on him, ripping to shreds the thicket right and
left and smacking in the roots. The Lieutenant Colonel
paid no heed to this, nor had his messenger warned him
of it.

Just then, Adolph Hitler sprang forth along with
a comrade, and both blanketed their commander with
their bodies. The Lieutenant Colonel was held up in the
lookout and asked Hitler amazed: "What was that for?"
– "We will not lose our Regiment Commander!" was
the humble response. With a silent handshake the
Lieutenant Colonel expressed his thanks.

Three days later the company leader was at the
regiment command post meeting, in order to receive the
company's battle orders. For lack of space Adolf Hitler
and the other messenger had to desert their dugout for
a short time. Artillery salvos struck again and again
upon the dugout, whirring and howling roars of
exploded debris everywhere, crumbled earth rained
down.

Then it roared again nearby – the immense
crashes – a direct hit in the middle of the regiment
command post!

Adolf Hitler was one of the first to rush down to
the rescue. A bloodcurdling scene presented itself to
him. The dead and wounded lay under the rubble.

Quickly, his eyes searched for the Lieutenant Colonel. Was he also dead? Then he saw through the black smoke his commander sunk down with a moan, and was immediately at his side. His right leg was red with blood; a shell splinter had lacerated the artery.

Here, only quick help could bring salvation, and Adolf Hitler did not deliberate long. He found a large strip of moss, laid him with his leg above the wound and wrapped him with telephone wire to halt the strong bleeding. The provisional dressing was apt and fulfilled its aim. Courageous stretcher-bearers carried the severely wounded through heavy enemy fire to the field hospital.

So Adolf Hitler saved, through his prompt, prudent help, the life of his commander. Lieutenant Colonel Engelhardt recovered again from his severe wounds and repaid loyalty with loyalty.[82]

The Iron Cross First Class

The company leader held his binoculars again and again and saw across to a bombed out barn to where the German lines were situated. Yesterday, the French shot so savagely on the farmstead, and today it was entirely calm over there. "Private Hitler, go at once to look there, and take a man along with you!" Cautiously, Adolf Hitler along with his comrade crept toward the house and found all to be quiet. Hush

---

[82] *Treue mit Treue*

down! – Halt! Abruptly they heard voices in the cellar. Quickly Hitler sprang down the stairs towards it, opened the door a crack and cast a view inside. The cellar was filled with a horde of French. Now there was only one goal: to not panic! Hitler flung the door open entirely, drew his pistol, and yelled in French: "Hands up! Drop your weapons! You are captured."

The amazed French cast their weapons aside, ascended the stairs and stood outside. There were 20 men! They found out too late that two German soldiers had captured them.

As Hitler and his comrade returned to their regiment with the many French, there was great delight there. For this act Adolf Hitler received the Iron Cross First Class.

Comrade Hitler

The heaviest barrage fell upon the trenches of the List Regiment. There, all of the telephone wires were destroyed, and only through crews of men could messages be delivered. Thus the messenger in the dugout of the Regiment Commander must at all times be at the ready. One of them was the Private Adolf Hitler.

Now, should an important message need to be brought to the forward battle lines, the commander would command the messenger, whose turn it was, to ready himself to go. He then gave the man directives, how he should best go through the barrage to reach his target, and the other messengers concerned would also give him information and comradely advice.

But during these conversations enemy fire always became stronger, and hence the regiment commander determined to first wait for a calming, before the carrier would report.

Adolf Hitler had up until now been in the tight quarters of the overfilled crew dugout sitting silently. But now he said suddenly: "Give me the message!" – "Why? It is not your turn", retorted the commander. – "I know the terrain well", answered Adolf Hitler, "and can bring the message safely forward."

He took the slip of paper from his commander in his hand and went quickly along the difficult way through the pelting barrage. After his return he reported soberly, that he had executed his orders. – On the next day a shell pummeled the entrance of the dugout and induced bad casualties. Among the wounded, Adolf Hitler himself was found. Now he saw his homeland again after a long time. And when he was hardly healed, he sent a telegram to his regiment:

"I have been released from the hospital for two days and would like to return again to regiment. I will not be in Munich while my comrades lay with the enemy."

The Fight in the *Hofbräuhaus*

The World War had come to an end. Traitors and Jews had given the enemy power over the German people. Now Adolf Hitler would save the German people from demise. He founded and led the NSDAP and orated as speaker in many meetings.[83]

Adolf Hitler had called, for the evening of November 4th, 1921, a mass meeting of national socialists at the *Hofbräuhaus* in Munich. His opponent, however, planned to crash it at all costs.

The *Führer* himself depicts in his book *"Mein Kampf"* the evening: "As I, at quarter to eight, entered the vestibule of the beer hall, there could certainly be no doubt as to the existing intention. The hall was overcrowded and therefore had been closed by the police. Our adversaries, who had appeared so early, were located in the hall, while our supporters were for the most part outside. The small S.A. detachment awaited me in the vestibule.

I had the doors to the large hall closed and then called the forty-five or forty-six men to step up. I made it clear to the young men that likely today they would for the first time bend or break for the movement,

---

[83] Adolf Hitler did not found the NSDAP, but it may be creatively stated here because he gave it its final name.

uphold their loyalty, and that none of us must leave the hall, except if we were carried out dead; I would remain in the hall, believing that not even one of them would leave me; but if I should see anyone become a coward, so I would personally rip off his arm band and take away his insignia from him. Then I called upon them to advance at the sight of the slightest attempt to crash it and then to bear in mind, that your best defence is your own offense.

A threefold *heil*, that sounded rougher and hoarser than usual, was the answer.

Then I went into the hall and surveyed the situation with my own eyes. They sat in there, packed tightly, and sought to pierce me with their eyes. Countless faces with dogged hate turned toward me, while others again, with jeering grimaces, let out unequivocal shouts. They would today 'make an end to us', we should watch out for our guts, they would shut our mouths once and for all, and all the rest of these lovely phrases. They were aware of their superior power and felt correspondingly.

Still, the meeting could be opened, and I began to speak. I always stood on the long sides of the hall in the *Festsaal* of the *Hofbräuhaus* and my podium was a beer table. I found myself, therefore, in the midst of the people. Perhaps this fact bore responsibility for always allowing a mood in this hall like I have never found anywhere else.

In front of me, rowdy enemies were sitting and standing. There were robust men and young chaps throughout…[84] Along the left side of the hall they had pushed in front of my table, and began now to collect beer mugs, that is, they ordered beer again and again and set the empty mugs under the table. Great batteries came into being, and it would have left me in wonder if the matter had concluded well today.

After about half an hour – so long could I speak despite all the interruptions – it appeared as if I would be the master of the situation. The leaders of the invading troops themselves seemed to also feel this; for they became more and more disquieted, often going out, coming in again and talking with visible nervousness to their people.

A small psychological error I made in the defence of my speech from an interruption, and which I myself having barely got the word out of my mouth had become conscious of it, gave the signal to strike.

A few wrathful interruptions, and a man sprang up suddenly on a chair and roared into the hall

---

[84] The textbook omits a very small line in the book *Mein Kampf* that elaborates on the factory associations of these men. The line should read: "There were robust men and young chaps throughout, in a large part from the Maffei factory, from Kustermann's, from the Isaria Meter Works, etc."

'Freedom!' At which signal the freedom fighters began their work.[85]

In a few seconds the whole room was filled with a roaring and screaming crowd, over which, akin to howitzer shells, innumerable beer mugs flew, in between the cracking of chair legs, the bursting of the mugs, bawling, howling, and screaming...[86]

I remained in my place, standing, and could observe how completely my boys fulfilled their duty.

I would like to see a bourgeois meeting like that!

The dance had not yet begun, as already my Storm Troopers, as they were called from this day on, attacked. Like wolves they launched themselves in packs of eight or ten again and again on their enemies, and began little by little to actually thrash them out of the hall. Already after five minutes I hardly saw one of them who was not streaming with blood. How many of them there were I had only come to know at that time; at the cusp my brave Maurice,[87] my present private secretary Hess and many others, who, already gravely hurt themselves, attacked again and again, so long as their legs could hold them.

For twenty minutes the hellish crashing lasted, but then the enemies, who perhaps must have

---

[85] This seems a sarcastic reference to the German Social Democrats.

[86] The textbook omits the phrase "It was an idiotic sight."

[87] Emil Maurice was an early leader of the Storm Troops.

numbered seven and eight hundred men, by my not
even fifty men, had been for the most part beaten out of
the hall, and chased down the stairs. Only in the back
left corner of the hall there remained still a large cluster,
and offered bitter resistance. Then suddenly from the
hall entrance toward the podium fell two pistol shots,
and now wild shooting began. One's heart nearly
jubilated in view of such a revival of old war
experiences.

Who shot, could not be understood from then on;
the only thing one could establish, that from this
moment on the fury of my bleeding boys might had
swelled and finally the last disturbers, overwhelmed,
had been driven out of the hall.

It was about twenty-five minutes that had
passed; the hall itself looked as if a shell had struck it.
Many of my supporters were being bandaged, others
had to be taken away, alone, we were to remain the
masters of the situation."

The conductor of the meeting[88] exclaimed: *"The
meeting resumes. The speaker has the floor"*, and Adolf
Hitler spoke again.

The Blood Flag

---

[88] Why the author chose to end the quote and rewrite the last sentence almost
identically to the original wording in *Mein Kampf* but with the omission of Hermann
Esser's name is unclear. By 1941, the date of this book's publication, Esser had
become a rather obscure figure.

Hardship and despair dominated in the German peoples. The French and English still held the occupied Rhineland. Millions of Germans had no work. Jews and treasonists did all the talking in the newspapers and in parliament. The governments were cowardly and helpless.

Yet Adolf Hitler sought to turn over this hardship. He wished, with his friends, to form a new government and to unify the people in resistance against the enemies within the land. In Munich he had negotiated with the government of Bavaria, and it seemed a few men would help with this government. As Hitler presented his plans in a manifesto, huge rapture predominated. But on another day the Bavarian government was also against Hitler. The men, who yesterday had promised to help, broke their word and became betrayers. Because of this, Hitler would lead the people himself. He decided hence forth, to be the head of a march through the streets of Munich. On the 9 of November at 12 o'clock noon, he set the SA[89] and the *Bund Oberland*[90] from the *Bürgerbräukeller*[91] in motion. In front the swastika flag was carried, then followed the top brass, there was beside Adolf Hitler, also General Ludendorf, Captain Göring, Dr. Weber, the leader of the *Bund Oberland*, and Alfred Rosenberg.

---

[89]The *Sturm Abteilung*, the Storm-Troopers of the early Nazi movement.

[90] A nationalist organization that in 1929 became the Dachau Nazi party.

[91] The *Bürgerbräukeller* was a cellar of an inn in Munich. It was one of the favorite gathering places of the NSDAP.

Already in *Ludwigsbrücke*, which had been closed off by the border police, they tried to stop the march. But the policemen were unarmed, and under the hurtling jubilance of the population the marching column moved irresistibly through Thal to *Marienplatz*[92], bent on *Weinstrasse* and straightened again through *Berusastrasse* to *Max-Joseph-Platz*, from there, rushed by near the *Residenz*[93], to gain *Ludwigstrasse*.

At the *Feldherrnhalle*[94] again stood a strong police detachment that wished to force the march to a halt. But now there was no stopping it. By hook or by crook, the march for freedom must be finished, no matter what the sacrifices should be. In the blockade-chain of police fell one command – and now the terrible occurred: German men, who in exercise of the trade of soldierly duties, fired upon the German Freedom Movement, at the pinnacle of which marched Adolf Hitler and the General Quartermaster of the World War![95] Unmerciful rattling of salvos on the march pressed close together, and many National Socialists weltered in their blood. Adolf Hitler incurred in a fall a collar bone fracture and a shoulder joint injury, his true companion Ulrich Graf, who had flung himself as a shield for his leader, took many bullet piercings, and was altogether seriously

---

[92] The square at the medieval heart of Munich.

[93] Presumably the King's *Residenz*, historical meeting place of Bavarian Kings.

[94] A memorial to fallen German war heroes, acknowledged by some to be the "spiritual centre" of Nazism.

[95]While they may have fired at Hitler, no soldier shot at General Ludendorff as he marched right past their lines.

wounded. Göring fell with a serious gunshot wound in the lower leg. Fourteen[96] heroes lay dead on the pavement. The flag, reddened from their blood, was rescued. It, as the "Blood-flag", has become the holiest symbol of the movement.

Hitler was carried by car to *Uffing am Staffelsee*, where he was arrested the next day. The dream of German freedom shone unrealized.[97]

So the deaths of November 9 became the first martyrs of the National Socialist struggle. Many followed them and had likewise sacrificed their blood and lives on the altar of the fatherland. But they were the first. The struggle was mostly at the time unpromising than in later years. Thence there was also their greater mission. They rendered for the world the proof that this new movement was ready, with the blood of their fighters, to conquer the path to German freedom.

The *Führer* had the sixteen[98] fallen of the 9th of November hauled out by marching column, the "Comrades, shot dead by the Red Front and Reactionaries" and set them in the *Ehrentemple* in *Königsplatz* at Munich in a memorial, that through the simplicity and nobility of its form professed testimony

---

[96] There may have been as many as sixteen Nazis killed in the Putsch. Reports range between fourteen and sixteen.

[97] *Der Traum der deustchen Freiheit schien ausgeträumt zu sein.* There is no English equivalent for the German word *"ausgeträumt"* but the word is often used to express disillusionment or resignation for the present political situation. A more literal translation might be "the dream is over."

[98] Why the number changes to sixteen in this paragraph is unclear.

to the greatness of their sacrifices and at the same time for the value that they meted out to the movement. Thus, their mortal remnants of the 9th of November 1935, in their unadorned graves, scattered in passed-by cemeteries in Munich and surrounding area, were taken out and after darkness were laying in state in the *Feldherrnhalle* to be transferred on the next day in a solemn march to their new tomb.

Accordingly, they became forever the "Eternal Guard," and this day would be remembered for coming generations in perpetuity.

A Storm-Flight

On an April day of the year 1932 a severe thunderstorm clamored over Germany. From black clouds pelted down hail and rain, and the storm-wind uprooted the strongest giant trees.

Adolf Hitler hurried in a car to *Mannheim* airfield. During the great election he coursed by airplane from city to city and spoke sometimes on a single day in four to five gatherings. Out of the airfield, standing in pouring rain, the most unshrinking of his adherents gathered; for they would remain nearby, when their *Führer* himself entrusted the airplane in such thunderstorms.

Nobody else risked flying on this day. The *Lufthansa* had totally discontinued traffic. But Adolf Hitler ordered takeoff, without even a blink of an eye to deliberate. In like time he would congregate in *Düsseldorf* with some one hundred thousand, who the *Führer* would see, and they should not be kept waiting for nothing.

As the airplane emerged from the hangar, it could only be held down with the crasser fists of the fitters and S.A. Men, by the utmost exertion of force, that the storm wind should not upset and smash it. The motors pounding, a short uprising, and verily the airplane swept over the area, inside in the witch's cauldron of the hurricane. Presently, down-gusts set in on it on the way, first it skittered through wispy clouds then it emerged from an invisible vortex in the depths, like being heaved by a gigantic violent crane. Hail and rain pelted on the outboard wing.

In this wild clamor of the thunderstorm the unshakable repose of the *Führer* was conferred to all of his companions. With suspense, Adolf Hitler followed the tough struggle of his pilots, and looked alternately at the map and clock. Then he had but only one worry, to not stray off course and to not come late to the next gathering.

Finally it was accomplished! On the Rhine the clouds broke, and through a rainbow the plane glided toward its goal. The storm-flight is lucky.

The 30th of January 1933

In Berlin before the *Reich* Presidential Palace on *Wilhelmstrasse* an immense crowd was jammed. Shortly before 11 o'clock the *Führer* with Herman Göring is driven up before the House of the aged Field Marshal and President von Hindenburg. Ten thousand hands have given the Nazi salute stretched toward him. Minute by minute elapsed. At once, movement came to the people. Göring bolted out of his car. Beaming, he called to the world: "Hitler has become *Reichs* Chancellor!"

There was breathless quietness at first, but then the masses boomed like a storm wind, a single outcry of jubilation sounded out: the *Führer* is *Reichs* Chancellor! Hitler is *Reichs* Chancellor, fate has entirely turned to the better!

"Now Hitler flags wave over all streets!" The goal of freedom has exploded, finally the oppression of the brown and black battalions, unconcern for failure or persecution thirteen years long that had railed against the courageous, gave way.

Outside before the *Kaiserhof*[99] the crowd had been growing to a hundred thousand. From all back streets they pressed forward, in order to see the *Führer*.

At 5 o'clock the new government met. On the side of the *Führer* sat no longer the captain, but the *Reichs* Minister Herman Göring, *Reichs* Minister and Provisional Minister of the Prussian Ministry of the Interior, at the same time Commissar of Aviation. A

---

[99] Nazi headquarters at the time were located in *Kaiserhof* hotel.

ceremonial feeling beheld all ministers around, as Adolf Hitler next for the first time as chancellor of the German *Reich* spoke to her mangling, put his course clear and allotted statesmanlike tasks.

High moods dominated in the streets of Berlin. The first brown battalion pulls through the streets overnight in a torchlight procession.

It had become night, but the jubilation had not stopped. The festive mood had been reproduced over all of Germany. In Berlin in the area of the *Tiergartens*, the SA and SS, the Steel Helmet and the patriotic associations, coming in all directions of the capital city, organized in a torchlight procession. Dull sounded the drumming from the Brandenburg Gate here. On *Wilhelmstrasse* and on *Wilhelmplatz* stood an immense crowd. No little place is free. Here, not a needle more could drop to the soil. The lead of the march turned about with a hundred thousand torches on *Wilhelmstrasse.*

Shocked and pleased about this profession of a people again freed and felicitous, the old venerable General dwelt at the window of the brightly-lit *Reichs*-chancellery. In the annex stood still at a window of the new *Reichs*-chancellery the man, who now received the thanks of the entire people, the man, who doggedly, never became weak in unrelenting struggle, who always steadily saluted the banner, when others dithered, who he and his people, whether in fortune or misfortune, always remained true, the leader of the

German people, its Reichschancellor, Adolf Hitler. Beside him Herman Göring and all the supporters, who were at his side in struggle.

Sturmbann[100] by *Sturmbann* drew past. *Wilhelmstrasse* droned from the step of the battalions, who reveled in the new freedom. As their step long faded away, there clustered outside from the windows of the *Reichs*-chancellery another hundred thousand men.

For years the National Socialist warning cry "Germany, awaken!" had attempted day to day and night to night to rouse the German heart. Now, the German people awoke. The Field Marshal of the World War, the current *Reichs*-president, has entrusted the unknown private of the World War Adolf Hitler with the leadership of the people.

A Small Parcel of Earth

Adolf Hitler broke the first ground, and with it the grand work of the *Autobahn* began. On the building site, in front of an embankment, the *Führer* spoke to his workers. Then he gripped his spade and moved up the track. A convoy of trucks rolled over, large, with entirely filled trolleys. With hard blows they tipped their loads out. Time and again the spade of the *Führer* drove into the clay. That was not a onetime groundbreaking, that was straight ground-work. A

---

[100] Battalions of the SS

couple workers realized that the *Führer* hardly stopped, before the pile of two cubic meters, was roughly spread out. They sprang forth with their shovels, in order to help. Laughingly, the *Führer* with both strange work-mates stopped, as there was no more to shovel, and went through the work site, where since then the work had begun.

"Have you seen", said one of the two work-mates of the *Führer* to the other, "how the *Führer* even shoveled the earth away from the track, so that the trolley could pull out again? What an upright ground-worker. That able labor, I can barely keep up!"

In the week following that first groundbreaking a supervisor came to the construction manager for the *Autobahn* and said: "Mister Foreman, we must surround the site where the *Führer* had shoveled with a fence! Our workers at the end of the day take parcels in their bags of the earth home with them. Also the women and children are fetching it."

Many a working-family from that region today preserves a small parcel of earth carefully as a precious possession.

A Quick Fulfilled Wish

In Hamburg a war invalid dragged himself through the barrier chains that cordoned off access to the *Führer*'s quarters. "I will bring a song to the *Führer*!" The SS-men sent the man through, and he composed himself off the street and under the window of the *Führer*, drew his instrument with quivering fingers on the gray shell and played a song. In silence and devotion the mass of many thousand beheld it. Sorrowfully the melody of the street musician drove in the ear of the *Führer*.

Adolf Hitler bade the man to come to him, spoke with him and heard the story of his life. "Four years I have been unemployed", said the war casualty near the conclusion, "can you, my *Führer*, not bring wages and work to me again?"

Then Adolf Hitler motioned to his adjutant. Two prompt phone-calls, - then the *Führer* said: "Report tomorrow to your new workplace, you can immediately begin work!"

Like wildfire the news spread amongst the waiting mass. Never ending, wild homage erupted as the answer to the *Führer*.

"Today they are all with me!"

The young worker troop mustered a great parade. The *Führer* steps the frontline and looks at each of the particular young men deep in the eyes.

He turned to one of the young workers: "Are you a party member?" – "No!" – "Are you an SA-man?" – "No, I belong to the worker's front." – "What were you formerly?" asked the *Führer* after a pause. The blonde young man lowered his eyes, righted himself then said stumbling: "I was a young Communist, my *Führer!*" To speak that was very hard for him. All eyes were now directed toward him. An embarrassing moment! Then the *Führer* took the hand of the young man, clasped him and said smilingly: "But today you are indeed all with me, my young people!" And blood red in the face answered the young worker: "By God, that you can depend on, my *Führer!*"

The *Pimpf*[101]

A fine sun lay on the marketplace of Erfurt, as the Hitler Youth, central Germany, marched by for the *Führer*. The houses all around the square were richly adorned with flags. Men were waving far out the windows and applauded with jubilation and hooting enthusiasm. A strong band had based itself in the middle of the *Freiplatz,* and under their marching music swarm after swarm, element after element, drew by the *Führer*.

There marched in the last row a follower with the youth, one *Pimpf* from the young people, an oddity in the row of the fresh, invigorated youth. A physically disabled child. The right shoe carried a swollen sole and huge heel, so that the leg was too short. The back was humped, and the head seemed too big for the frail body. With all strength the youth exerted himself, in straight poise to come about the parade route. How he got a

---

[101]Comparable to a Boyscout

grip on himself was impressive, and not so overconfident as to jab at his comrades![102]

The *Führer* noticed the *Pimpf* and gave him a long look. In the faces of bystanders there was dark pity to discern, and many a person asked himself why the boy was found in such a column. He could not at all stand exertion in the long run! – So, as the youth with his column gone is left in their dust, Adolf Hitler motions his attendant over and says: "Take the name of this youth fast! He gets my picture with my signature!"

Beginning of the Highway

On a Palatinate highway marched two *Arbeitsdienst*[103] workmen to the next city. Far in the country lay the *Arbeitsdienst* encampment, and far is the way to the train station. But both the men were in good cheer; at that time it was their leave, homeward bound, after months of healthy, arduous work. They sung to themselves: "At home, at home…" One motorcade now passed by both men. "That's a good idea", reckoned the one. – "It is faster than we are", said the other. – "Wave!" shouted both together. And with that indeed the motorcade stopped and waited, until both men, who set them-selves in a trot, were caught up. "Where from? – Where to? – Get in!" The both of them became round-eyed for astonishment, that who else on the

---

[102] *um von seinen Kameraden nicht allzusehr abzustechen!*
[103] The National Socialist depression-era "Work service."

highway had stopped and ordered two *Arbeitsdienst* workmen men to get on, than the *Führer*. He let them describe their life to him, and how it was in their *Arbeitsdienst* camp, so that he could know all the details. Then, they arrived at the small city. The vehicle stopped. In parting the *Führer* asked of one of the two: "It will soon rain; have you no coat with you?" – "I have no respectful coat, my *Führer*, I was so long unemployed." Then the *Führer* pulled off his gray travelling coat, and placed it on his countryman's shoulders. And before a word of thanks could be brought to him, the string of cars had already rushed off again.

The *Führer* wins back his Homeland for the *Reich*

It is the 12th of March 1938. In a broadcast, a proclamation of the *Führer* was read:

"I have myself resolved, that the millions of Germans in Austria from now on stand under the aid of the *Reich* and at its disposal. Since this morning the soldiers of the German *Wehrmacht* march on all the frontiers of German Austria… I myself as *Führer* and chancellor of the German *Reich* am lucky, for I from now on as a German and free citizen am able to enter this land, that is also my homeland."

At the lead of the troops hurried the *Führer* through the beautiful *Ostmark*. How long had this land had to wait for its homecoming to the *Reich*! Many before National Socialism had suffered through a martyr's death at the gallows. The *Volk*-traitorous Government in Austria had imprisoned thousands of German men and women. 40 000 fled into the *Reich*. 400 were slain and 2500 were shot in the bloody struggle of the *Anschluss* of Austria to the Reich.

Now this was all over. The *Führer* himself came. The *Volk*-traitors fled or were placed under arrest. Whereto the *Führer* came, the people exalted, ringing the bells. In Vienna he heralded: "As *Führer* and chancellor of the German nation and Reich I announce for history from now on the admittance of my homeland into the German *Reich*." (15th March 1938.)

And now the other Germans outside the frontiers in Bohemia and Moravia, in Memelland, in Danzig asked: "*Führer, when will you bring us home into the Reich?*"

The English and French would hinder this. But they would not risk war. Compared to the German army and the *Westwall* on the French frontier, they did not feel strong enough. The *Führer* negotiated in Munich with Chamberlain, the Prime Minister of England, and Daladier, the Prime Minister of France. The *Duce* of Italy, Mussolini, supported the demands of the *Führer*. England and France gave way.

So could the *Führer* continue his work again. The *Sudeten*-Germans turned home into the *Reich*, the Memelland became German again. As the then Czechoslovakia disintegrated and Slovakia became autonomous, Bohemia and Moravia turned back as protectorates under the protection of the *Reich,* to which they belonged for long centuries.

The *Führer* by his Troops

The English hastened to war and inveigled Poland and France to attack Germany. Thus Adolf Hitler called the *Reichstag* together. Adolf Hitler appeared in the *Reichstag* meeting in a gray field jacket. He announced his decision, to take lead of the troops in war. In his speech he called the name of his successor in the event that anything should happen to him. As the older, well tried World War soldier the *Führer* saw his place in this campaign nowhere else as by his troops.

The *Führer* at first joined the troop divisions, who in the Corridor territory were breaking through the Polish front and surrounding strong Polish troop divisions. The countenance of the *Führer* heightened the jubilation of the troops of the Vistula, thrusting up over the high Kulmer. The fate of the northern Polish army is sealed, it is doomed.

Having concluded the campaign in West Prussia, the *Führer* searched out the Silesian army group. They are pushing in a northeastern direction. In an airplane he observed in the midst of battle west of the Vistula from Kielce-Radom the operations and the retreat of the beaten Polish army.

The *Führer* is always there, where his soldiers stand in deciding battles. And finally came the day that was said: cease-fire! Warsaw had given itself up. Also the *Führer* came to this place. In conquered Warsaw marched the victorious by their sovereign warlord, their "first soldier".

Anywhere, wherever the *Führer* appeared, he was greeted with hurtling jubilation. No more beautiful moment was there for officers and soldiers as those, in which they could stand and report for their sovereign commander, only by him to become great. In depth the *Führer* conveyed all the time the valiant caution of a solitary soldier and made various troop division dispatches. The feeling that the *Führer* with his headquarters in the middle under the warring troops founded in the frontlines spurred all on to the highest of power.

How Warsaw was Conquered

At Warsaw a Polish army of 110 000 men had withdrawn.

Desperately it tried to force a breakthrough in the East. But its efforts were futile. The valiant German troops resisted all Polish attempts at a breakthrough. Ever tighter, ever steady, they closed the ring around the city.

In order to avoid the demolition of the state, the *Führer* allowed the surrender of the Commandant. But in arrogant terms the Pole deprecated. Also, the second offer, the complete evacuation of all women and children out of the city, he disobeyed. With 110 000 soldiers and about 1 million inhabitants he vowed to defend the city, and with that he knew, that in few days the food would be exhausted. So the German army management made another proposition: all foreigners (about 1200) should be removed from the city. Only with reluctance did the blinded Polish Commandant act on this offer. The foreigners left Warsaw and were well escorted through the German troops and guided to the north.

From a water tower the *Führer* overlooks the city. He knows what fate now is immanent for her. All supplies cut, it already lacks bread and meat. Nevertheless, the Polish general thinks that the city could still be defended. He has ordered anti-tank ditches built. Each house should be a small fortress. Razor wire, and on the outskirts buried mines, should annihilate the attacking Germans. But the breadths of anti-tank ditches do not only cleave through the streets; they also interrupt the water, gas, and lighting lines and the sewers. In many city districts there is already no water, no gas, and no electric light anymore. The fire brigade could not intervene if a fire broke out.

Still one last time the *Führer* asks the Commandant to invite a hand-over – in vain! Now the battle must begin. While the *Führer* returns back to Berlin, in order to brief the *Reichstag* and to once more offer the enemy a hand in peace before he affects upon Warsaw a hard, unrelenting fate.

With the airplane attack on the 24th of September on military installations, the battle begins. Uninterrupted German planes crossing over the city throw their heavy bomb-loads down. The droning of the motors emerge now from the left, now from the right as a conglomerate of dive-bombers swoop overhead. More huge fire clouds rise up; brighter firelight shines through the air. Ever-new sources of fire come into being. From the more numerous scenes of fire rise clouds of smoke that rejoin themselves into one gigantic black cloud-wall and darken the afternoon sun.

From the front yards and fields all around Warsaw the muzzle-flashes of German guns tremor in short intervals: light and heavy Howitzers, mortars, and long barreled guns, between heavy and light anti-aircraft batteries. The firing and impacts clang many times in the housing blocks and form a prolonged thunder and grumble. Still the Polish guns answer back; still the Polish anti-aircraft guns send their exploding shells into the air. Then the opposition trails off. As the evening approaches, the German air raid peters out. The *Führer* has forbidden a night raid, in order to spare non-military targets. But the German artillery battles on. Their direct hits destroy the fortified installations. Munitions depots fly in the air. Sources of fire build upon sources of fire.[104] Battle groups on battle groups

---

[104] *Brandherd reiht sich an Brandherd.*

bring ruinous bomb loads upon fortifications, block streets, gas utilities, arms factories, and waterworks. They turn back, for a second, a third time with heavier bomb loads to launch. The black cloud wall over Warsaw grows and grows. Over the city comes annihilation.

While the artillery barrage still clamors, the infantry regiments, on the 26th of September, step on to the forward line. An upper *Pfälizish*[105] Regiment penetrates through with hand-grenades, pistols and bayonets step for step in a suburb. After embittered house to house fighting, some forward positions of fortifications are captured. In like time the Silesian Regiment from the Vistula and the East Prussian territorial-army formations from the North close the ring tighter and faster. On the 27th of September the German pressure intensifies so much, that the Commandant determines that negotiations had to begin. A Polish envoy arrives at 08:29 hours to the German high command. The fire remains sparse afterward. The city is poised to turn over power. Now, after 5 days the transfer of power of the city can follow. Firstly the roadblocks must be dismantled, the mines removed, and the forces of the Polish Army amassed. Then march 110 000 Poles in captivity. They leave a razed city, a hungry population, behind.

---

[105] Denoting the approximate area of the former governmental district *Pfalz* in the Rhineland-Palatinate

With the fall of Warsaw the last Polish resistance is broken. The remaining strongholds have already strung-out the forces. Now comes the surrender at Modlin of both Polish armies. The battle in Poland is victoriously finished. In less than 3 weeks the German troops have defeated a strong military adversary. Poland has ceased to be a state.

On October 5th the *Führer* arrives in an airplane on the airfield in Warsaw.

One honour-company of the army and the *Luftwaffe* reported on the airfield. Many of the soldiers carry on their breast the proud medal of the Iron Cross. General von Brauchitsch, General von Rundstedt, General Milch, the General von Reichenau and Blaskowitz, the Flight Corps Generals Löhr and Kesselring as well as the newly appointed German city-Commandant from Warsaw, General Lieutenant von Cochenhausen, stand on the right wing of the honour-companies. Nearly all carried the Knights Cross of the Iron Cross.

As the *Führer* left the cabin of the airplane, the companies present, the generals report. And while the *Führer* paced up and down the front line, the national anthem sounded off. Then the *Führer* made his way in the city, to where a fir-decorated podium stands. Hurtling jubilation sounded out, as he drove, with flags through the decorated streets of the greater German *Reich*. Now he is at his goal. From the podium, from the great and luminous place of the *Reichs* war flags, he awaited his troops.

And then they come up, the campaigners for Warsaw: infantry, cavalrymen, engineers and pilots, newsmen, and *Panzer* formations. Many of them are decorated with the Iron Cross, some of them with the Iron Cross First Class, a couple with the brooch of the Iron Cross First Class. Twice have they struggled for this high distinction, the Iron Cross First Class of the World War and the Iron Cross First Class 1939. Never would they forget marching past their topmost commanders in Warsaw.

The *Führer* as Commander in the West

After the defeat of Poland the *Führer* again and again sought to end the war. But England and France did not will peace. They will destroy Germany. Their troops should infiltrate through Holland and Belgium taking over the Ruhr valley. That, the *Führer* knows to prevent.

On the 10th of May 1940 the German troops bit the enemy in the wide front of the Western frontier. The *Führer* himself has taken to the front, in order to direct the battle and advance.

Under his leadership the German *Wehrmacht* gained the greatest victory that has ever been. All of Holland and Belgium become occupied after hard battle. The French and English must flee. A million man army of prisoners fell into the hands of our soldiers.

The *Führer* has his campaign plan so laid out, that the general of the French and English did not expect it. He lets the adversary break through the front, and with help of mechanized troops they succeed to surround and destroy the adversary. Again the campaign goes, like in Poland, with greater rapidity forward. Paris becomes occupied, and our Troops penetrate the south to the Spanish frontier and in the West to the shores of the Atlantic Ocean. On the 21st of June the *Führer* took to the forest of Compiegne. There, in 1918, as the World War came to an end, a German delegation had asked for a cease-fire. The French had handled the German General with villainy and abuse. In remembrance of that, the French have displayed in a hall, the railway car in which their General in 1918 received the German delegation. Here the French erected monuments as a reminder of the disgrace and for the French to make hate against Germany.

On the 21st of June, 1940, at 15:00 hours the honor company marches here on the memorial site of German disgrace. At 15:15 hours the *Führer* arrives at this monumental place. The leading men of the *Wehrmacht* receive him here. The *Führer* steps under the sound of ceremonial marches at the front of the honor company. Then he boarded the car with his entourage.

At 15:30 hours the French delegation appears. A General notifies the *Führer* of the French envoy. Then these people enter the car.

In the car the *Führer* and his entourage briefly rise. The French greet the *Führer* and then likewise take their place.

The chief of the Army High Command of the *Wehrmacht*, General Keitel, rises and reads off the order of the *Führer* and High Commander the foreword to the cease-fire terms. Reminded in it is the nefarious behavior that in the year 1918 was meted out to the German representative. At the same time however, the *Führer* lets the representative of France open in the foreword: Germany does not have an intention, as the French might expect, that would compare with the disgraceful behavior of their despotism in the year 1918.

Following, the translation of the foreword is delivered through Envoy Schmidt. Shortly thereafter, the *Führer* with his entourage leaves the car, while General Keitel remains with the French authority in the car and with them negotiates over the terms of the cease-fire.

As the *Führer* reaches the memorial place, the chief of the honor company notifies him: "My *Führer*! The Pan-German *Wehrmacht* greet their High Commander!" The *Führer* reciprocated, the anthem of the nation rings out.

The *Führer* steps with the High Commander of the *Wehrmacht* divisions at the front, while those members of the French delegation remained in the car and rise from their places for the play of the German national anthem.

Before the *Führer* climbs his car on the end of the forest path, the General Field Marshal Göring brings to conclusion this historic hour a trebled *"Sieg-Heil!"* of the *Führer* and High Commander. – The disgrace of the 11th of November 1918 is effaced, an old injustice on the German people is again made good.

On the 22nd of June 1940 the OKW[106] gave notice: "On the 22nd of June, at 18:50 hours, German daylight savings time, in the forest of Compiègne, the German-French cease-fire contract was signed.

The undersigned took forth: On the German side as representative of the *Führer* and High Commander of the *Wehrmacht*, General Keitel, of the French side as representative of the French government General Huntzinger."

So the *Führer* effaced the disgrace of 1918.

---

[106] *Oberkommando der Wehrmacht* – The Armed Forces High Command

Horst Wessel, Fighter and Activist of the Movement

This Wessel is right!

For a couple of years, the student Horst Wessel was a simple S.A.-man. Often he stood at that time on three or four evenings a week in the somewhat large hall in Berlin as "Hall-guard". Then, the Communists had to be fended off; they always sought to disturb the meetings.

That was an arduous service. But Horst Wessel went also to the meetings of the Reds. If there a Communist held a long speech, about how good would be the fare of workers in a Communist Germany, then Horst Wessel would stand up and volunteer a word. And now he said a reply to the Communist: "It is all swindle. Germany would be run into the ground, if the Communists have any say, and only Adolf Hitler can help the German worker!"

At first the Reds in the meetings were entirely numb to the effrontery of the Nazi. But if they wished to then "bump" him off, as they call it, he was already gone.

Horst Wessel soon remarked that most men like to hear when he spoke. And so he talked often in all kinds of meetings. Afterwards, an entire crowd of men would step up to the Nazi Party, because they thought: this Wessel is right!

Shot by the Red Front

Quite weak from a long, hard convalescence in his parents' house, Horst Wessel taught during the evenings in his room back on *Frankfurter Strasse*. He lived there with Witwe Salm, a Communist, who the red front infiltrated, to spy what information he could about their master. Horst's SA comrades had requested often, for their *Führer*, who feared for his life, to search for new accommodations, and finally Horst gave in to their solicitation. So he said now to his host that he was moving out and began to back his bags.

Meanwhile the wife of the house hastily walked over to the nearest Communist pub, where the most notorious hoodlums of the Reds sat together and played cards. "The Nazi hound, this Wessel, is here again! Go! Now is the time, we can ice him! He is all alone at home." They threw their cards aside and stopped their powow. They had long sworn revenge against Wessel because he recruited so many workers and led them to Adolf Hitler.

Quickly Witwe Salm was sent to another bar to get more muscle; and when he came back with more chaps, they all went out, 16 men strong, to *Frankfurter Strasse*. Their group leader was only just released from prison.

At the front door they had one member of the band remain on the street, to keep lookout; the other conspirators will sneak into Witwe Salm's kitchen and discuss once more the scandalous plan.

Horst Wessel was in the middle of packing when he heard a noise. He thought it was an SA comrade so he went to the door. "Come in!" he said and opened it. The crack of a shot – in the mouth, and Horst collapsed – the cowardly murder squad made their escape.

People ran to the house from the *Sturmlokal*,[107] the comrades came and brought Horst to the hospital. There he laid for a long time near death. His mother and sister sat in trepidation by the side of his bed; Dr.

---

[107]The local precincts of the *Sturm Abteilung* (SA).

Göbbels came often to see Horst and each day asked the SA Comrades how their leader was doing.

Finally an improvement came in his condition; the bullet was removed from the neck, and the wound started healing. All were glad that Horst was saved when sudden blood poisoning set on and all the doctor's work was in vain.

The SA Comrades asked if they might be allowed to see Horst one last time; and as the doors to the hospital room opened, all of them saluted their group leader with the Hitler salute. Horst could not speak anymore, but his eyes expressed his joy.

Horst Wessel died the next morning in the arms of his mother and sister and went in great death throes, falling for the sake of a new German *Reich*.

Herbert Norkus, Loyal until the Death

The Enemy

Herbert Norkus whistled a farmer's march to himself and stepped steadily out to make it to the social evening[108] of the Hitler Youth. As he came about the *Beussel* Bridge, he was stopped suddenly by the Communist Klingbeil, a seventeen-year-old chap.

"Hey, Norkus, why're you not coming to us? Know what ya need, yer too strong a youth to pretend to be a spit-bowl[109]. Should give you time to think. But consider the matter now. Either you come to us or..."[110]

He held his fist under the nose of the youth. "Who don't come to us, Norkus, we bash their head in. The brown stuff should be turned red. No others have worth, and can use some bloodstains. So consider that. In a week, have an answer for me." Herbert stood still. Thus was the enemy! Now he looked him in the eyes; the struggle could begin, the opponent knew him now.

Klingbeil was already a few steps away, as he once again came back to the petrified Herbert standing there, grabbed his shoulder strap and said: "You fancy these rags?" – Then Herbert came alive. "Do not

---

[108] *Heimabend*

[109] A derogatory reference to the Hitler Youth's brown uniforms.

[110] This quoted speech is written in a Berlin working class dialect. The intention is to show the Communist to be unintelligent.

wrinkle the uniform! And with that you know it, I will never come to you, never! Our goal's name is Germany! For the traitors we spit." – Herbert spat out for the flabbergasted Klingbeil – "You have no hope, that in eight days my opinion will be any different than today. I am a Hitler Youth and know what I will do!"

"Shrimp, make me listen to your prattling!" screeched Klingbeil, "We will not hear from Hitler." Herbert could barely contain himself: "You haven't the slightest notion who Hitler is and what he will do. He will free the people, will free Germany again and make it independent!" "When you don' come to us", threatened Klingbeil, "then guard yourself! We've won with your motha, your fatha ran to us, and with you, who is not ready so fast. Brown dog – guard yourself! But there's still time, in eight days we speak again!"

Herbert remained still for a moment. In the heart of the fifteen-year-old youth lay the agony of a life or death decision. Steady, he began again and eventually arrived, quite late, to the social evening.

Put to Death

On Saturday evening the *Kameradschaftsführer*[111] Gerhard Mondt ordered: "Early tomorrow we will deliver a leaflet to the houses. I'm sorry, but I must pull each of you out of the sack right at 05:30 hours. But we

---

[111] A junior leadership rank in the Hitler Youth. It would literally translate to Comradeship Leader.

will certainly not come weekdays. All of you sleep until this time Sunday and we will be well able to deliver the leaflets without trouble. I will be working with: Gerhardi, Kirsch, Bauschus, Kirschner, Norkus."

The youth spent the night together with Mondt. Thus on Sunday morning at 05:30 they would all be ready. Gerd Mondt went onto the streets first, the others always stayed 20 meters behind. All, obviously, without uniform, in civilian attire. It was a wet, cold, foggy January morning.

On the side of the street Mondt pushed away a chap who came at him suspiciously. Under the lantern he recognized him as a Communist chief. Slowly he went on prudently, so that the operation should not be a failure. No, that would not do for him; the youths found it to be ungrounded. But he would resume the delivery of the leaflets on another street. There he stood and Gerhardi Wache watched the others as they delivered, two on the each side of the street. When they suddenly saw a Communist on a motorcycle with no lights drive by, Mondt knew what that meant: within five minutes the whole block will alarm with whistles and signals, and the delivery work will meet a disagreeable end. He made a hasty retreat, and the distribution resumed on another street.

First all is quiet. Then came a newspaper boy passing by, who both the lookouts did not recognize. It is the brother of Klingbeil...

Soon after a troop of about 30 Communists arrived on the corner and marched toward both of them. When in this moment Norkus and Krümel came from a house, they gave Mondt a signal to quickly take-off. They understood also, and Mondt thought he was safe. In between, Mondt and Gerhardi were surrounded by the Communists. Mondt drew his pistol and let off a warning shot in the empty street. Gerhardi could escape, Kichner and Bauschus, hearing the shot, escaped as well. With his gun Mondt halted the Communists in this game of chess, until he thought all of his comrades had gotten away. Then he fled himself and disappeared in the fog.

In between, Herbert Norkus finds death on *Zwinglingstrasse*. He is not successful, as his comrades were, at getting himself to safety. One chap remained constantly on his heels. He fled. The Red murderers seized him, but he strained and tried again to reach the door of the *Hansa* dairy. But to no avail, the big iron door, which was always open at this hour, was now locked tightly. The fog was hintering Herbert's efforts. He moved up to the dairy and reached to the latch, but he could not open it, because someone had bent the key inside of it. Now he had only one last chance, if the Reds were not as fast to get to him. In his fear of death, he headed to the schoolhouse door, but it was Sunday and the door was locked.

That was his last hope, he could not try any longer. All alone, Herbert faced the onslaught of the knife-wielding mob. Repeatedly he was struck to the ground as he tried to run. But always and doggedly he defended himself and with his hard fists struck out , hurtling more and more strikes through the air. The effort made him tired, and the blood-lust was relentless. There is a lamp-post, there he can stop, there he will not fall down. But there the jeering gang pulled him right to the ground and trampled on the defenseless victim. He saw the glint of knives and felt sharp stings. One more thing occurred to the youth and he stumbled to a Laundry; but this door was locked too. The last thing Herbert heard was Klingbeil's voice: "Now, brown dog, now fight the rest!"

In the alley beside the store he was beaten. There Herbert succumbed. Everything goes so dark for him, the blood runs in his eyes from his face. He crawled through the alley toward the door to the apartments. His hand reaches for the handle but he blacks out. He has lost consciousness, and where he lay, with each heartbeat, blood ran from six stab wounds.

This is how his friend Krümel found him, who had stopped in a neighboring safe-house. He brought him to a hospital; but Herbert Norkus was no longer conscious. He had offered his young life for Germany's resurrection.

Paul von Hindenburg, the General of the World War

The Testament

When Paul von Hindenburg was still a small youth of 10 years, his mother gave him a bread roll each morning to take to school. He noticed once, that one of his schoolmates had nothing to eat, and he asked him: "Did you have no breakfast?" The other shook his head: "My parents are poor and can not give me any." Then and there Paul pressed half of his breakfast into his hand, and thenceforth he brought with him each day a bread roll.

But one day Paul had to leave his parent's house. He should become an officer, and thus he had to go to school in another, remote city. But for the farewell, he made his testament.

There sat the youth for his great acting assignment, read out the testament, and gave away all his toys to brother and sister. His poor schoolmate he had not forgotten; then the Testament ended with the words: "My brother Otto should take to Schreiger a bread roll every day. That I have written this true and truthfully, this is to certify."

Tannenberg

The Russians were occupying east Prussia. The
Kaiser had entrusted General von Hindenburg, who
was already in retirement in Hannover, with the
command of the Eastern Front. It was an emergency. At
night he drove there from Hannover. In Marienbrug
Hindenburg with his General Staff chief Ludendorff
were keen on the local population, who were concerned
with the advances the Russians had made. "We were
trusting of one another and united in the effort to do
our parts," as it says in Hindenburg's daily orders.

Hindenburg thought over the situation; then he
concluded not to withdraw or he would be annihilated.
First, the one Russian army, then the other. The entire

German army in the North East must regroup. A great
march and many train transports were necessary. The
movement of the German army was difficult. But when
the German troops surrounded the Russians, the
cavalry pulled far into the second Russian army. But
Hindenburg did not lose his composure now. He stood
by his plan. He now came to a great battle. Day and
night there was fighting. But soon the Russians were
exhausted. They donned white flags and gave up.
Thousands of abandoned horses, ammunition dumps,
machine-guns, and supply wagons fell into the hands of
our troops. Ten thousand prisoners were disarmed and
brought to prisoner of war camps. And when the
prisoners were driven forth in the darkness of the night,
the gratitude and victory songs of the Germans rang out
over the whole battlefield; now all thanked God.

Hindenburg did not rest on his laurels. He struck
the other Russian army in the Masurian Lakes. Again
over 100 000 prisoners were taken. East Prussia was
thus freed and the advance to Poland could begin.
Hindenburg drove forward until occupied Russia had
been freed. Such a fight of utter annihilation, as the one
Hindenburg had won in Tannenburg[112], had never been
seen in all of history. Now with one action Hindenburg
had won the admiration of the whole German people.
He was thus appointed the Commander of the whole
German army by the *Kaiser*.

---

[112]The Battle of Tannenburg actually took place near Allenstein, but was named after
the Battle of Tannenburg (Günwald) to compensate for the German defeat there in
the year 1410.

Two Words

One time the *Reich* President Hindenburg received the representatives of the many political parties that existed in Germany at the time. As he was bidding farewell to the gentlemen, Hindenburg said: "My Lords, I have so often heard from you the word 'Party'. I miss the word 'Fatherland'!"

Albert Leo Schlageter, a German Hero

A Snowball Fight

On a beautiful winter day the teacher hikes with his youths out into the forest to have a snowball fight. The one half of the class occupies a hill under the command of the teacher, the other should attack this hill. Their leader is the ten-year-old Albert Leo Schlageter.

With cheering the youths storm the hill, but they do not come far. The flying snowballs from above are too dense. "Retreat?" thinks Schlageter. "Impossible!"[113] Suddenly, he springs forth entirely alone up the hill, runs between the legs of the teacher and pulls him fearlessly down from above. His fellow combatants jubilantly storm after, and the hill is conquered.

The Artillery Observer

The Battle of Flanders raged. There the village of Warneton is a smoking ruin, only the church tower juts above the whole land. However, it is also badly damaged and is seriously slanted. At any moment it could collapse.

---

[113]Nazi military doctrine relied heavily on the idea that retreat was forbidden. Every propaganda effort was made to ensure the idea was not in the German lexicon. When, late in the war, the Germans were vastly outgunned, a retreat was euphemistically referred to as "an attack to the rear."

Through the drumfire Schlageter sprints over debris and wreckage on the way to the tower, up the half-charred stairs and sits on the roof. From here he can best direct the fire of his battery.

"Too short!" he looked back. - "Too wide!" the next salvo misses. And now it unrelentingly strikes the enemy lines, round after round, the English positions were battered. It hailed down with fantastical exactitude, for the availability of good observers was rare.

Then the tower was struck hard by a shell. Slowly it leaned to the side. Schlageter searched now, as the tower would soon collapse, for a way to escape. But it was too late to be; his comrades must grab him out of the pile of debris. When they found him it was only by a miracle that he was unharmed.

An Expedition

Schlageter, after the end of the World War, fought in the Baltic lands as a volunteer for the German *Freikorps*.[114] Hardly had the war ended, when a war broke out against the Poles in Upper Silesia.

The Polish standoff is in preparation. One must gather secure intelligence on them. Schlageter takes on the mission, to get clarity on the situation, and rides with a bicycle out in the darkness to the Polish positions in Upper Silesia.

---

[114]*Rettung des Deutschtums.*

Throughout the streets there are guards: civilians with red and white armbands and rifles. He was stopped, made up a sound excuse and asked around on the street. Perhaps he could find a vehicle here to get a ride with.

"Wonderful!" thought Schlageter. "One travels in speed and comfort to his destination." He sat with a harmless sightseer with a cigarette in his mouth on the street as a vehicle came. Its crew was armed with rifles.

"Hey, can I get a ride?"

The truck stopped, and one of them asked him where he was from and where he was going. "The chap speaks perfect German", they thought, "it is better for him to come with us than to let him walk around."

"Jump on!" Schlageter did so, but they did not take their eyes off him. Their rifles were always at the ready.

Schlageter examined his opponents with the most harmless expression, and saw more than he had expected.

The vehicle drove off the road toward a farm where their lead vehicle, seeming to be harmlessly driving across the land, was loaded with rifles, machine-guns, and ammunition. Then the young fellows would deploy on the street. The weapons were distributed evenly among them. Now Schlageter knew that the standoff would be coming soon.

But how would he make his way back and bring the news? He came up from the head troop, where through his persistence he managed to sidle out of any serious questionings. But someone sent two cyclists after him on the road. "How can I lose these chaps?" thought Schlageter. "We will search, with the strongest legs and the best lungs!" The most wild chase of his life began. Very quickly Schlageter stopped off, so that one of the pursuers crashed. The other raced by, jumped off and left his bike on the road. Then Schlageter ran up the street – and escaped to freedom. The pursuers had met their end.

How Schlageter Freed German Prisoners

In time during the Polish standoff in upper Silesia, the city jail became over-filled. Among the prisoners were 21 young Germans, who had offered their lives for the honor of the fatherland. They were brought out from there and put into French prisons.

Schlageter and his comrades heard of this and conspired to free the prisoners. Quietly they rushed from cell to cell and awoke the sleepers who could hardly believe their luck at being liberated. In between was the prison commandant, a Frenchman, who was startled out of his sleep and was tied to his bed.

First all is quiet – then quickly hard shots ring out through the still. Now speed is the key. The liberated were loaded in two waiting vehicles, then they went in wild driving pushing the vehicles to their limits. From time to time a bike rider would appear in the headlights who were in collusion and gave the sign: this way!

Both trucks reached the German area before the enemy even knew what was actually happening.

Schlageter and the French

As Schlageter escaped pursuers in Poland, he unexpectedly ran into a troop of French soldiers. A couple people purposely threw hand-grenades at them to make an end to them. The enemy was fainthearted and raised their hands up.

They were prisoners of Poland now who would not let them live. Schlageter, however, dispersed his people in every direction and allowed the French to escape. So he saved their lives.

The French, later, would murder Schlageter!

Shock Troop Schlageter in the Ruhr Battle

From *Mülheim an der Ruhr* a small troop of men slunk along unassumingly dressed towards the south. Carefully they moved through the towns and streets; if someone saw them, and found the explosives – then all was lost.

As the dawn approached, they got nearer to the train tracks that ran throughout the forest. The track could be blown up, and the French went through this stretch, since they had to get to the Ruhr area, to get the stolen coal to France. Now the stand is here!

The night is pitch black. Quietly Schlageter moved over the field; but there are no enemy guards to see. Step for step, Schlageter moved, creeping forward. Now he found the embankment – there, where it crossed a stream.

Then suddenly the stretch of line lit up and glared. A spotlight! He dropped to the ground, and did not move a bit, until the light went away.

Now it's on! Two boards were brought out fast – explosives on them, across the boards, the fuze was set – ready! "To the second rendez-vous!" urged Schlageter. There! A shattering thunder! A second! - Schlageter smiles contentedly – the bombing is successful.

The train tracks are destroyed, and for many weeks the French can not use the track to transport their stolen coal back.

Schlageter's Death

At the crack of dawn there was a French cavalry troop sent to the prison in Dusseldorf. The door opened. Two policemen walked around, between them Schlageter, - walking expressionless, upright, and proud. Following them was a German minister, his aide, and a German lawyer.

The prisoner, along with the two policemen and the three Germans climbed aboard a waiting truck. It drove slowly through the city toward Friedhof, to *Golzheimer Heide*. The Chaplain read Schlageter the last rites that his wrinkled hands clutched.

They descended their way into a sand quarry. Screaming music shattered the silence. Three companies of French infantry marched out and presented arms. In the center of the place stood a lone post, ten meters away from it there was a group of 12 soldiers standing at attention.

All eyes were trained on the convicted who emerged from the wagon with his escort. Upright and unshaken he looked them in the eye and gestured with his hand: "Give my regards to my parents and siblings, my friends, and my Germany!"

With steady steps he goes to the pole. Quickly a clerk reads the sentence. Now Schlageter must kneel at the pole. A French soldier binds his hands and feet and blindfolds him. Then a loud order! - Rifles clank. The officer lowers the sword. A crash, the salvo fires. Schlageters body falls over. An officer goes up to him and shoots Schlageter through the head. Albert Leo Schlageter is no more!

He gave his people the best thing he could give: he offered them himself.

Manfred von Richtofen, the Red Baron[115]

The First Englishman

Germany had many valiant pilots already in the World War, and one of them had already shot down dozens of enemy airplanes in air battles. Manfred von Richtofen was assigned to a newly trained fighter squadron that served under the command of the famous fighter pilot Boelcke. Brand new machines were arriving. On the next day, for the first time, they would be used against the enemy.

Boelcke had continually in the last days "for breakfast", as he said, shot down at least one Englishman. But all the other pilots of the squadron were still amateurs. None had so far one hit to record; thus they all burned to succeed in the eyes of their leader, in the first honest test.

On a clear September morning the Boelcke-Squadron ascended out to battle. As the Front was reached, an English squadron of seven airplanes emerged, and Boelcke flew to it with his four comrades to cut them off and engage. Only a mere second, and it began! Richtofen did not deliberate long and took to the next Englishman at once, a two-seater, off the front sight. Both adversaries shot, but at first without a hit.

---

[115] *Kampfflieger* – I chose to substitute "Baron" for the original German because of the familiarity of English readers with this nickname. The German literally translates to "Combat Flyer."

Because Richtofen could only shoot in the direction of his flight, he had to maneuver after it to come behind the adversary. The adversary now knew that his last hour had come if the German was on his back. So twisted both airplanes with full power in frantic circles here, each trying to reach a position above and behind the other.

Now the battle depends on who has the greater calm and knows the right moment to seize. Richtofen had only one thought: "The adversary must fall, come what may!"

All of a sudden the enemy flew a short stretch ahead, and already the German sat on his tail. Now it was sealed! Quickly Richtofen rammed the Englishman, so close came his machine to him here. Then suddenly the propeller of the enemy airplane turned no more. The motor was shot, and the adversary had only one option remaining, to land in German territory, as he could no longer reach his own lines. From the faltering movement of the airplane it was clear, that the leader must have been hit; and also that the observer could no longer see, as his machinegun jutted without direction in the air.

The Englishman landed in the vicinity of the German aerodrome; Richtofen went down next to him and ran up, in order to look after the adversary. Both occupants of the enemy airplane were badly hurt and died shortly thereafter.

They were honorably buried, and Richtofen decorated the grave of the valiant adversary with flowers and set, to their memory, a stone on it.

"Such a man we will never see again"

Again, Richthofen started out with his squadron. He flew over the Front and searched behind the lines for enemies, until he found a strong attacking English squadron on the offensive. During the fighting Richthofen noticed several of his comrades were lingering too long in enemy airspace and were not able to break off. He dove to them, not upon a particular opponent, in order to intervene, to quickly bring the enemy under fire to help each of his comrades.

Then suddenly his plane's motor cut out. A breakdown? Or was it hit by a bullet?[116] It was unlikely now to reach the friendly front, and so Richtofen slowly began to glide lower.

A young pilot[117] who was on the front for the first time and had only been in small air battles noticed this. He did not understand who he was facing and that the

---

[116]The engine failure story was invented by a German newspaper soon after the incident. There was no sign of damage to the engine of the plane, however. This story, while not a Nazi invention, may have been used by the Nazis to save face on the Red Baron's defeat. It is notable, however, that the worst fabrication, in which a few Canadian soldiers shot Richthofen in the head upon landing, is absent from the story here. This book predates German hatred for England which intensified after the strategic bombing of German cities, and peace is still thought to be possible between the two "Racial Allies." England is portrayed as honorable.

[117]The book is alluding to Lt. Wop May, the young pilot the Red Baron was chasing when he was shot down.

enemy was defenseless. He dove after Richtofen's plane, which could not evade, and took the first deadly shot.[118] After 80 air victories the "Red Baron" found a hero's death. His comrades were gripped with horror, as they saw how Richtofen's plane went under. They could not help and had to bring back the terrible word that they had returned home without their leader. -

With all military honors the English buried the "Red Baron."

The enemy pilot, afterwords, who had killed Richtofen, wrote in his war chronicles: "I felt miserable and unlucky. There lay Richtofen, the greatest of all! If only I had been able to say to him how much I admired him in life. Such a man we will never see again."

---

[118]This account is completely wrong, even for what was known at the time of this book's publication. It was the experienced Capt. Roy Brown, and not Lt. Wop May who was thought, at the time, to have shot Richthofen. Richthofen was actually chasing May at the time, not vice versa.

Otto Weddigen, the Captain of U 9

U 9

The English had, in the World War, barricaded all Germany's trade with their large fleet and wished to starve Germany. So Germany fended and dispatched U-boats out, in order to destroy the English ships. The commandant of one of these U-boats was Otto Weddigen.

Captain Weddigen went to the base, and always paced the deck of his submarine U 9 up and down. Twenty steps there and twenty steps here he could make, then he was at the tower or forward at the nose. Every now and then he remained standing there, shot a glance with his hand against the rising sun and looked over the endless expanse of water all around him. At present he had been on patrol for several days in English waters and had until now no enemies to face. Slowly, the boat broke and sank in the swell. Up in the tower stood the watch, an officer and a sailor, who with their binoculars searched the uninterrupted horizon.

Just as Otto Weddigen descended into the boat, the sound of a cry pealed from the tower: "Smoke ahead!" Like lightning the commandant was up again and peered through the glass, straining his eyes. The cloud of smoke spread out, high masts appeared underneath, and soon there was no more doubt: an English warship drew near!

"Dive, quick!" – the shrill command was like a release from a long rest. Each ran and tumbled to his post. The portholes thudded, water whooshed into the ballast tanks, machines sang with a flurry of sound, and soon the deck of the boat was immersed in the flood.

Impatiently, the Commandant looked at the depth gage, while his hand clamped the handle of the periscope. Finally 10 meters of depth was attained.

"Lower the periscope!" commanded Weddigen. Tense, he searched over the water surface, and his voice quavered with arousal, as he cried out: "Wow! Three enemy armored cruisers – straight ahead of us!" Then, however, he had again been firm in power. Calmly, he gave his order: "Bring in the periscope! All torpedoes clear to shoot!" After a short time the bow and stern area[119] replied: "Torpedoes clear!" – Ever nearer slid U 9 to the enemy ships, now the first cruiser was only about a hundred meters away.

"Attention! Fire Torpedo! Lower the periscope!" commanded Weddigen. Against the calm sea he had to go around especially cautiously with the tip of the periscope, should he not be discovered. According to the highness of the waves that ran over the boat, he motioned with his right hand the periscope up and down, while the left turned after the enemy rearing down. Now the bow of the cruisers ran in the crosshairs

---

[119] *Bug-und Heckraum*

of the periscope ahead, now the stern, the mast and now – the midship!

"Now!" – The watch officer pushed off the electric contact knob of the first tube. An easy tremor in the boat – the torpedo was out!

"Bring in the periscope! Depth rudder!" – Weddigen's eyes goggled at the hand of the stopwatch. The seconds became eternities. – Then suddenly a hard metallic crash… and then one cry in the boat: "Hurrah!"

Shivering for the hungry uproar the Commandant ordered that the periscope be gently brought out. And as he looked through it, it shone in his eyes. The English cruiser was sinking, its stern was already immersed. Lifeboats floated all around, men jumped into the water – but Weddigen's gaze was already directed upon both of the other cruisers.

"They must be frenzied", he said quietly to himself, "they lie stopped next to the sinking ship!"

In full calm Weddigen continued the second attack on the first prominent cruiser and likewise shot two torpedoes upon it. Both met; the powerful ship capsized hard on its side and sank within a few minutes.

The third opponent now came on. Out quite a further distance Weddigen fired both of his rear torpedoes out at it, but only one met the target, and he seemed to have damaged the ship only lightly. Thus U 9 turned the bow anew onto the enemy. Then a torpedo, the last, vacated the tube, and fetched its prey. The armored cruiser thudded; its bulk, with red color painted under water section wallowed and glistening out of the water, and with hundreds of men, who desperately searched for a foothold, as it sank gurgling in the flood. Three large armored ships Weddigen had destroyed with his small, antiquated submarine.

With struggle and hardship U 9 escaped the enemy Destroyers that stalked it, and brought safe and intact the tidings of the great victory to the homeland.

Weddigen's Last Tour

On a new tour with U 9 Weddigen succeeded once again in sinking an English cruiser. Then he was named the commander of the submarine U 29, and soon he was again under way against the enemy. Although U 29 had no deck guns on board, it could stop five merchant ships of the enemy and annihilate them through *Sprengpatronen*.[120] The energetic appearance of the German commanders struck the enemy Captains with such fear, that they could not think at all of resistance or flight.

After the rich razzia U 29 again navigated to the homeland, as it suddenly split open the main body of the English battle fleet. Three battle squadrons loomed there, and immediately Weddigen took on the first enemy ship. The English were put on guard. He took the periscope of the submarine and also saw a few

---

[120] Small copper bombs with a 5 to 10 minute fuse used to destroy merchant ships.

moments later the trail of a torpedo pass close by his stern. Instantly the squadron swerved away and tried to escape the enemy. But Weddigen remained obstinate and came forward to a new attack.

Then suddenly pealed the cry from one of the English line ships: "U-Boat right ahead!" Some hundred meters away someone had sighted a periscope, and immediately directed the enemy battleships toward the opponent. Weddigen could no longer reach the needed depth in order to evade the impact. So the English navigated with full force to the flank of the German submarine.

For a short moment the bow of the ramming boat loomed steeply on the surface; then there was only wreckage and a large oil spill visible.

Otto Weddigen had, with his brave crew, found a hero's death.

Bismarck, the Forger of the *Reich*

The First Medal

One afternoon Lieutenant von Bismarck stood in conversation with other officers on a bridge that stood in the vicinity of Stargard over a lake. Meanwhile his stableman Hildebrand rode a horse to the watering hole, right by the bridge. Suddenly, however, the horse lost its grip on the ground, it turned over, and Hildebrand plummeted under.

As Bismarck saw that, he immediately drew his sword, tore his tunic off, and sprang headfirst into the sea. He snatched the stableman luckily; but the drowning clasped his rescuer so recklessly, that he had to go first with him to the bottom in order to get himself off of him. It succeeded, and Bismarck drew buoyant his servant, who had become unconscious, and himself after, onto the bank. Hildebrand came to again, and was healthy on the next day.

For this act Bismarck received the *Rettungsmedaille*, and that was for a long time the first medal that he had carried.

Once he was asked, at a time when he was decorated with many more medals, what the humble votive medal with the yellow ribbon actually meant. Then answered Bismarck with a serious look: "I have the habit sometimes of saving a man's life."

Throwing People Out is my Thing!

After his first state examination, Bismarck assisted the judges in the courthouse in Berlin. One day he interrogated a man that he found irritating because of his imprudence. Bismarck sprang up and turned to him: "Sir, pay attention, or I will throw you out!"

Then the attending courthouse council tapped him on the shoulder and said in a whisper, censuring him: "Throwing people out is my thing!"

Then the questioning went on. But it was not long before Bismarck thundered to a renewed boldness of the man: "Sir, you better pay attention, or I will let the Honorable Court Council throw you out!"

Bismarck, the Forger of the *Reich*

In the year 1815, as Germany was finally becoming free from the servitude of Napoleon, the Emperor of France, Bismarck was born. It had been a half century, in which many Germans had struggled to unite the German people in one state. But it did not succeed. The provinces of Austria, Bavaria, Saxony, Hesse, and all the many small and smallest states remained independent. They would subordinate themselves to no-one, and also France and the Hapsburg Emperor did not want Germany to become one.

But when Bismarck became a minister in Prussia and his political career began, there were also many of the people who were against him in uniting Germany. He would not allow traitors, do what they may, the enemies of Germans, hinder the might of Germany in Europe. The members of the legislative assembly would not grant him the money for an increase in the army. Thus Bismarck had many, many opponents and only few friends. But the King trusted him.

Bismarck appealed to his King:

"I have this dream, where I am riding on a small Alpine path, to the right a chasm, and to the left a rock face. The path is getting narrower, so that the horse is unsteady and hesitating and becoming unnerved. I strike the rock face with the switch in my left hand and appeal to God. The switch becomes infinitely long, the rock face falls like stage scenery and there is a bright, open path, a view of hills and tree-lines, with Prussian troops with flags. In the dream the thought came to me, that I could briefly tell your Majesty."

With the Prussian troops that he had now without the assent of the legislature, Bismarck had persuaded the Danes to return Schleswig and Holstein. And as the *Kaiser* of Austria refused to cede it, Bismarck took it by battle as the Prussians, through Bismarck, became stronger and shaped a German *Reich.* In the year 1870, through Bismarck, all German territories unified in war against France. And as the war was won, due to the success of Bismarck a united German *Reich* was founded.

It was the 18th of January 1871. The thunder of guns hailed on Paris. Far and wide resounded the cheer from the Palace of Versailles. There, with four black horses pulling open wagons, as he traveled every day, came the King of Prussia, Wilhelm I, to Versailles. He was led by the crown prince through the columned hall and up the marble stairs to the Hall of Mirrors. There the Prince stood on a high platform in the room behind the King, surrounded by the flags of the fighting regiments. Bismarck now made the proclamation in which King Wilhelm promulgated the unity of the *Reich* and the accession to the throne.

Jubilant spirits prevailed. Without regard to rank or position they all rushed to be the first to congratulate the Kaiser on the rebirth of the *Reich*. From the towers of the palace, the Prussian black and white flag was replaced by the black and double red *Reich* flag.

Bismarck had, through wise politics and dauntless courage, realized this feat.

Blücher, the Forward Marshall

A Rude Parting

Blücher became Cavalry Captain by promotion and wrote to Frederick the Great: "He who is of a hunter's origin, who has no other merit than to be the son of a Margrave of Schwedt, is preferable to promoting me. I beg your Majesty for my leave." The King gave him nine months detention, so he would have time to reflect.

As Blücher however remained unfaltering and renewed his letter of resignation, the King wrote: "The Cavalry Captain von Blücher is dismissed from his service and can sheer himself to the devil!"

Blücher and Nork

The French had, under their *Kaiser* Napoleon, occupied all of Germany. Now the King of Prussia, the *Kaiser* of Austria, and the *Kaiser* of the Russians united in order to expel Napoleon. The German people were levied for a struggle for freedom. In this liberation war General Nork led a huge troop unit in Blücher's army. Blücher would plan the best moment to attack the French. For these reasons his troops must march far and long, for reasons they could not know. Nork could also not see the reason, and at once he went rudely against the Field Marshall. The former, however, answered even more rudely, so that Nork asked the King to assign another army unit.

As Blücher was questioned about Nork, he answered: "I beg for you only to leave the old Isegrim[121] to me; we will soon be rightly making merry. If he growls at me, then he will bite the French even more sharply. He is a picture-perfect General who I can always depend on."

After a great victory Blücher reported to the King: "The uncompromising valor of the troops, your majesty, became futile when Nork was not the *führer*. Not myself, only he, deserves the honor of the day. He is not my friend; but I tip my hat for this great combat General."

The Forward Marshall

In the morning before the great battle of Katzbach, Blücher rode in the pouring rain and drove his troops on the saturated soil forward. "See, my beloved children," he turned to them, "the rain is our old ally here from Katzbach. Today we will save the King lots of gunpowder!" "But we will waste more

---

[121] A mythical Wolf-like creature from German folklore; he symbolizes the feudal Baron in both positive a negative senses: ruthlessness, strength, viciousness, greed, and foolishness.

flasks, father Blücher!" answered the people, laughingly.

Eastward stumbled the column despite insuperable hinderances. "Children," urged the elder, "I have promised assistance to my English comrade Wellington, and he would not want me to break my word!"

But the soldiers overcame all quagmires and all temptations to grumble. Then Blücher dismounted his horse and waded in the mud next to the young gentlemen. "I say, we must go on, children! Do they hear how the cannons come booming across from us? And now, when Napoleon sits so pretty in his high office, should we let such a little bit of muck stop us? Are we their scoundrels?" - "Nee, that will not be – viva the old Blücher!" was the answer. Without rest they went on with all their strength to fight, to win the next battle.

Ferdinand von Schill, the Fighter for Freedom

With six Men against the Enemy!

The Lieutenant Schill had only barely healed from a bad wound, when he rode to Kolberg, in order to help defend the city against the approaching French. He volunteered himself to the Commandant of the fortification and asked there, to set troops at his disposal, so that he could obtain provisions from the surrounding area. The Commandant gave him – six men.

On the same day Schill pulled out of the city with his armament. In Treptow he found out that the French were advancing. That did not suit his plans; for he wanted to undertake a raid, not a hopeless skirmish. Therefore, he sent in two of his cavalrymen to engage the enemy and let the rumor out, that the Russians had landed at Kolberg and would attack the French by stealth. –

The guile succeeded, the enemy was terrified and withdrew. In complete calm Schill now hoarded a great heap of provisions and brought it to Kolberg.

As he then made a report to the Commandant, he asked also about reinforcement for his small flock. But his wish was refused. So the even six had to make do and carry on.

The Last Battle

Major Schill, with his troop, had been pushed back to the fortress of Stralsund. There he would endure his last battle.

With overwhelming force the enemy attacked the fort, whose fortress structures soon fell, overran the walls, and poured into the streets. There the battle raged one against one. Schill readied his soldiers: "If each of you is saved; so be it; should each of you die; so

you will die with me!" And the brave stayed and
fought, until they fell. -

The enemy thought the battle would soon be
over and the Colonel and the brass moved in regimental
columns in formation. Then Schill slapped the flanks of
his horse who snorted and sprung forward with his
saber onto his opponent. "Dog, give me quarter!" he
yelled, and the enemy Colonel fell from his horse with a
split skull. Now on all sides the Major fought and felt
his skin pierced. But he had a gash on his forehead, and
in a moment his vision went black, and he swayed in
the saddle. Until now he had the upper hand. The bold
ride went through umpteen streets. He must go east to
the rear, to wipe the blood from his head that was
obscuring his vision. He looked like a cadaver. The
enemy was forced back from him – a shot fell! - Schill is
fatally struck and falls from his horse. Soldiers bring the
body to the town hall and lay him in a hall on the
outermost bench.

The French General let the occupiers of the
houses, in which Schill had lived go free if they revealed
where Schill's body was. This Lord, a leading Swedish
officer, spoke to the General with cautious words in
French and thanked him for freeing the city from this
"bandit." Then the Frenchman sprung up and spoke
woefully: "Schill was no bandit, he was a hero!"

So the enemy honored his courageous fallen
opponent.

Joachim Nettelbeck, Kolberg's Saviour

How Nettelbeck became a Seaman

When the small Joachim Nettelback was eleven years old, his fondest wish became fulfilled. He was allowed to make a voyage on his uncle's ship from Kolberg to Amsterdam.

In the great Dutch harbor the lad saw a mass of stately ships about that had come from lands afar; then he grappled with the longing, to one day make a voyage into the wide world. From then on one could say he was a true seaman.

As he confessed to his uncle, that he would like to go on board of a great Indian voyage, he only reckoned: "You are indeed wrong-headed!" But Joachim did not give up his plan.

On a dark night he slipped clandestinely in the tethered dingy, cast off the cordon, and drove to a ship, that on the next morning would go to India under sail. Of his articles of clothing and additional things he did not take anything with him; so that one should think that he is drowned. Then one would not think to search after him on the other ships.

Quietly and cautiously he rowed up to the great ship and clambered on board, and afterward he bumped his boat back with his foot and it had drifted off to its fate.

Soon the entire ship's crew assembled themselves around the youth and asked from where he came and what he intended. Instead, each answer provoked the small Joachim to cry bitterly, that he feared, with scolding and shame, to be brought back to his uncle again. When one man took him to the Captain, he made a speech and explanation. And he had luck! Then after a short deliberation, the Captain said: "You may remain and come along as a shipboy. Monthly you will receive six *Guldens* payment." Then, a load was taken off his mind, and he joyfully worked in the company of the Captain.

Soon the ship went under sail, and the new shipboy set himself to work. But as he saw his uncle's ship become ever smaller in the distance, he became a little heartsick, and he almost regretted his flight. Under order of the Captain he had to write a farewell letter to his uncle; but it never reached its destination, and so the youth was thought to be missing. People assumed that he had fallen in the night from the boat, that people had hopelessly searched in the morning between the other ships.

Not until a year later did Joachim Nettelbeck return back from his voyage. Now he wrote from Amsterdam to his house, and one can imagine the joy of his parents, as they heard, that their assumed-dead young man was again alive.

A Ship in Peril

In beleaguered Kolberg the usefulness of the deficient cannons became evermore worse. Then came the heartening news that an English ship was nearing that had a great number of guns that were laden with the accompanying munitions. But because of the stormy weather the ship could not reach the bay; the crew had panicked in the danger and was stranded off the coast of Henkenhagen, and so it was possible that it would fall into the hands of the French.

Then Nettelbeck rushed to the harbor, in order to get advice on how the ship might be saved. As he went there, people were standing around, talking here and here, asking, consulting, and not coming to any final solution. The pilots would not navigate it through the stormy seas. They had much more to fear, however, from the French than they did from the high waves.

Nettelbeck exhorted and scolded more than a little, but it was all in vain. There occurred to him no other means, other than to embarrass the cowardly pilots, as he turned to the four of their wives. "Trine and the rest of you," he cried, "will you go with them?" - "Surely, sir, if you yourself go!" they answered. Now Nettelbeck took a pilot by the arm, in this instance of valor, took him in a boat, and sped out from Henkenhagen.

Nettelbeck had luck in reaching the English ship and brought it, with its precious cargo, unharmed into the harbor. In triumph 45 new cannons were installed in the fortress wall.

Soon thereafter, the King granted Nettelbeck's wish and sent a new courageous commandant, who through his wit, and with the help of the citizenry who defended the city for so long, fought until liberated Kolberg was freed of all tribulation.

Queen Luise, a Prussian Queen

The Forerunner

The small princess Luise went to search for her Grandmother, the countess of *Hessen*. There she played with the children of the servant staff and the farmers of the nearby village at the park of the castle, as suddenly a hard tempest with gales, lightning, and thunder came along. Quickly the mothers hustled the children over, in order to get them home; only one small girl, who did not have a mother anymore, was left there and cried. Then Luise bolted to her poor girl, took the child, and led it into the cover of the castle. "Wait here!" she said amiably; "Here we need have no fear. It will not be long, until your father will come to fetch you." "My father is not coming", answered the child sobbing, "for he can not go so far for me. He is a forerunner of the lady countess and must run here with others for her carriage, when she departs, and look after her, if she has no orders for him. The run injured him so much the last time that he always has an ache in his chest now. He will indeed not live much longer. – Oh, the pain, I may say no more of it all. My father has forbidden me strictly to speak of that, else he will lose his post." Luise comforted the poor girl, and put forth other thoughts, until the storm was over and the child could go home.

Then, however, Luise hurried to her grandmother and knelt down at her chair: "Grandma, I will tell you something that you should not know", and she told of it, what she found out and asked: "Can't you make it so, Grandma, to no longer let a runner for your carriage run ahead, not him and no other. He always laughed and appeared so friendly. But I have come to think that he looks happy outwardly, but he hurts in the chest and cannot breathe and will die." –

From this day the countess disestablished the forerunner in her court and allocated him to other services.

A Hard Task

In worried trepidation Queen Louise went to Prussia to a meeting with the Emperor Napoleon in Tilsit, to perhaps find a middle-ground on the horrible terms of peace. Her husband, the King, had asked for them, and she had not hesitated for a moment, to bring this offer. "Yes, I will go there," she said, "My people well deserve it."

When Napoleon made his visit to her, the riding whip held in his left hand, Louise emerged to him in all her Queenly beauty. He was struck and dazzled by her appearance; the Queen, however, had forgotten all of her fear and reluctance and remembered only the saving of her country.

"As a mother of my children I speak to you," she began. "We have gone through an unfortunate battle. You are the victor. But will you then exterminate us? Please have mercy, and receive our gratitude!"

But Napoleon interrupted the Queen with tactless words and inquired where she had her lovely dress made. "Your Majesty," answered Louise, "did we come here to speak of such trivial things?" So she pressured the Emperor to pay attention, and she asked him, to leave the most ancient provinces to Prussia. But Napoleon would not give in, instead he said irately: "Will we leave Prussia alone to wage war against me?" - Proudly and eloquently the Queen answered him: "We descend from the fame of Frederick the Great, and therefore we may fool ourselves with our power!" Immediately thereafter, the King of Prussia came into the room, and Napoleon was glad that the meeting could end.

With sadness Queen Louise had to leave Tilsit again, without having succeeded in the struggle for her Prussia.

Andreas Hofer, the Freedom Fighter in Tirol

Betrayal

Two times Andreas Hofer had chased out the French from Tirol, and the third time was underway. The enemy was master in the land, and so Hofer had himself, with his family and united followers, flee to the alpine wilderness. There he inhabited a lonely hut; but here also his life was not secure. The enemy searched after him and had placed much money on his head.

One day a farmer came to the French and said: "I know where this Hofer is." Then they gave to him the blood-money, and he led the French soldiers out into the high mountains.

On a starlit winter night, it was at four o'clock in the morning, a friend of Hofer's awoke in the hut. He eavesdropped beyond and overheard at one point, as he neared over the frozen snow in crunching steps. A man sneaked after, behind him a mob of soldiers with gleaming weapons. Now the French knocked at the door with their rifle butt. In a moment it became lively in the hut; but each opposing barrage was useless.

In the middle of the confusion only Andreas Hofer remained calm. They tethered his hands behind his back, put a cord around his neck, kicked him in the face, and roughed up his beard.

"In God's name", said Hofer, "now you have me." – the group hung him by arms and feet. "It is not kindly", he opined, "you are the stronger, that need not be established. I will come home again indeed!"

Then the French drove him away. Calm and upright Andreas Hofer stepped between them and looked neither to the right nor the left, until after he was locked in the dungeon of the fortress *Mantua*.

"Shoot Better!"

On a cloudy February morning Andreas Hofer was on the way to the firing squad.[122] As he was being

---

[122]*Richtplatz*, literally, the "place of execution."

collected from his cell by his escort, there was, outside on the steps, one of his compatriots and brother in arms, who had come in order to see his *führer* and comrade one last time.

Finally the gate was jarred open. For a while steps reverberated in the distance and came nearer in the hallway. In the half-darkness a Priest appeared with a glittering cross in his hand, behind him Andreas Hofer walked out, escorted under arms. The men stood like stone pillars. As they were now in the gaze of their *führer*'s eyes, they threw themselves on him, tied his hands and pushed him, weeping, to his knees. Hofer saw the pathetic sight. "Men!" he said to them, "to me it is great, that I may see you one last time! Go home! If you would do me a last favor, and give to me a shovel full of Tirolian earth on my grave!"

Outside, a horn echoed. Hofer rose to his feet and trod out to the firing squad. There, one could see his eyes. "That's not the custom," he said, "'tis not the first time I have stared death in the eye." And as he was summoned forward, and knelt low, he answered: "I will then, to those who created me, give back my very soul."

Then the officer stepped one step forward and ordered: "Fire!" - The first volley rang out; he flinched in the knee, motioned with his hand and yelled: "Frenchmen, shoot better!" -

The first shot of the second volley put an end to his life.

Maria Theresa, a German Matriarch[123]

"We die for our King"

Maria Theresa came to reign in the same year in Austria that Frederick the Great became King in Prussia. But now the powerful states in Germany and in Europe thought they could exploit the inexperience of the young ruler, who up until now was not allowed or could not look after the governing of the land. Frederick, the King of Prussia, advanced forth into Silesia. The Bavarians and French assaulted Austria.

From two fronts enemy armies advanced into Austria, Maria Theresa was advised in great emergency. So the young matriarch in this fatal situation where many would fail, set her only last hope on her ally, Hungary. One night she left Vienna in a travel carriage and drove on the bumpier streets in to Hungary to Pressburg.

There the aristocracy of Hungary convened, and there were many among them, who from the government of Maria Theresa, expected only disaster. So Maria Theresa appeared in the hall. She wore the Hungarian national garb, but not in the gay colors of joy, rather in the profound black of sorrow. On her head gleamed the crown. Calmly stepping, she mounted up the step, which led at the end of the hall to an elevated

---

[123] *Landesmutter*

platform. So all gave way to the courageous striking word and the brilliance and the magic of this miss, and the voices of malcontent silenced.

Maria Theresa, however, announced in the hall: "Of all destinations, I take my flight to you, to the forces and to the old gallantry of Hungary. I beg your help for my children and me. Hungary is threatened, my person is threatened, my children, my crown is threatened..."

Maria Theresa let her risen hand sink and inclined her head in deep emotion. So, like on an order, the assembled drew their swords out of their sheathes, and as if out of one mouth it sounded through the hall: "We all die for our King, Maria Theresa!"

So thus a Hungarian army railed against the enemy in the field and freed Austria from the great danger that had threatened it.

Service in Battle is Honorable Service

A particular solider had once mugged a shopkeeper and robbed him; he was not let off lightly by the judges. When Maria Theresa found this out, she wrote to the court: "Why was the soldier not hanged? It is a great honor for a Regiment to have a thief as a comrade! Not a moment longer will I think of having such a soldier in my army. Vermin with no honor should not be allowed to give honorable service in battle!"

"I have been mistaken"

As the Minister[124] one time did not agree with a decree of his *Kaiserin*, he wrote Maria Theresa a letter in which he set out his dissenting opinion and made other suggestions. To this, the *Kaiserin* repsonded: "My Minister is right. I have been mistaken, and in such an instance I see it so well, that my order was not practical and there were better alternatives."

---

[124]Likely the Prime Minister, Wenzel Anton von Kaunitz.

Prince Eugen, the Noble Knight

The Little Capuchin

The young Prince Eugen was brought up in the court of the Kings of France. One day he appeared before the King Ludwig XIV and asked him for permission to serve as an officer in the French army. So the King saw the lanky, pale youth and opined contemptuously: "He will become a soldier? Warriors appear anything else but as he. My officer must be a strong, powerful man, who must be able to endure all the hardship of war. – He knows that I will make a priest of him. Why does he not obey me?"
"I was born to be a soldier", answered Eugen with pride.

"Let them not laugh", countered Ludwig XIV. "He is and remains the small Capuchin." "So is my request therefore denied?" asked the Prince, and as the King nodded, he continued: "Then I will become an alien, from here forth, where anyone will need me."
"He will do only that!" said the King laughing. "He will be once again cheery, when he can come back to France, in order to become a chaplain."

So the Prince dismissed himself and went. Soon thereafter, however, he appeared in the service of the German *Kaiser*.

As Imperial Field Marshal Prince Eugen defeated the best commander of the French. So he gave the King of France great trouble, and the pernicious opponent was again brought to his side. He asked if the Prince would become a Marshal for France and be given much money for it.

But the Prince held Germany, that had admitted him, as his true fatherland and said to the French envoy: "Answer to your King, that I am an Imperial Field Marshal, and that is no less worth than the French marshal staff. I need not money. So long as I serve my honest master, I will be contemptuous of that."

The Forbidden Clash

The Turkish Grand Vezier was at the head of a great army invading imperial Hungary and was, afterward, on the way to Vienna to sack the city. The imperial army, that the Turks outnumbered greatly, was commanded by Prince Eugen. As they were going to wage a great clash against the Turks, they dispatched a messenger to Vienna to the Prince with a message requesting a war declaration. Eugen knew of the indecisiveness of the authorities and well anticipated it in the contents of the letter. Unopened he put it in his pocket and gave the order to attack; the clash ended with a fast and decisive annihilation of the enemy.

Right after the Prince opened the message from Vienna and found inside the order to avoid a clash under all circumstances, and that the army, the last hope of the *Kaiser*, must be preserved from defeat.

Prince Eugen appeals to the German Farmers in the Freed Danube Region

Prince Eugen, the old Knight,
would fight for the *Kaiser* again
City and Fortresses in Belgrade.
He would build the bridge
that no man could cross
with the famed army for the city.

Deutſche Bauern ziehen die Donau hinab nach Ungarn.
German Farmers Cross the Danube to Hungary.

As our German soldiers in this war had went against the Serbians, it was promulgated that there was to be a broadcast of the victory message in the first playing of the song from Prince Eugen. At one time the song sounded in all provinces of Germany. Farmers from the Black Forest, from Neckar and Moselle sang it for all. They spread and fiddled the fame of Prince Eugen, who had freed them from the Turks in the region of the Balkan German farmers. All along the way the farmers packed up their possessions. On pontoons and boats they crossed the Danube over from Batavia and Vienna. In Banat, in South Hungary, and in Serbia they found a new homeland, which would from today become German-inhabited. They built clean cities and villages and reclaimed swampland and dead land.

Frederick the Great

At Kolin

Frederick the Great waged war against the *Kaiserin* Maria Theresa. He wished to win Silesia for his land. With his army he besieged the city of Prague that was well defended by the Austrians. The *Kaiserin* Maria Theresa ordered her Generals: "Prague is to be relieved, cost it what it will." Frederick pulled with only a part of his army against the Austrians who would relieve Prague. Now a battle raged at Kolin. But the Austrians were superior. Frederick had no reserves. It was going so badly, they say, that he waged battle himself, sword in fist, with his soldiers against enemy guns, the unrelenting fire. But after great casualties his people gave way back from the murderous hail of iron.

Frederick did not mind this and rode along unconcerned through the rain of bullets. Then one of his officers shouted to him: "Will your Majesty conquer the battery all alone?" But now the King halted his horse, looked at the enemy cannons calmly through his binoculars, and rode slowly back to his. The siege of Prague was canceled, and the Prussian army marched away.

A Dragoon brought Frederick a drink of fresh water in his hat. He saw, how aggrieved the King was and said: "Now then, the *Kaiserin* can indeed win a battle once in a while, thereby we will not summon the fiend to come to us."

Frederick mustered his guard. Of 1000, 600 had fallen.

Now an evil time set on. The French, Russians, the Austrians and the *"Reichsarmee"* of the other German states moved forward against the Prussians. So the King wrote to his sister: "I am steadfast and determined, to do the ultimate, in order to save my fatherland. The freedom of Germany is at stake here."

"That is What I Stand For!"

The city of Greiffenberg in Silesia was destroyed after a terrible fire broke out and left the city completely in ruins. When Frederick the Great heard about the misfortune, he gave the Greiffenberger's much money, in order to rebuild their houses again.

Some time later the Old Fritz[125] traveled through Silesia in order to survey his land. There he found a delegation of citizens from Greiffenberg, sent to him to offer their thanks for his gift. The chief of the citizens stepped forward and began to direct the words of thanks to the King. Barely had he finished his speech, when the Old Fritz interrupted and said: "You have no reason to offer me your thanks. It is my duty to help my subjects. That is what I stand for."

Hang it Low!

Once, the Berliners regarded Old Fritz as evil, because he had raised the price of their favorite drink, coffee. So the King rode one day through the streets of the city, accompanied by only one servant. He saw from a distance, how the people had brought a placard and were posting it. As the King came nearer, he recognized his image on the placard. And there he sat piteously on a footstool, a jelly bag cap on his head and a coffee grinder between his knees. With his right hand he ground the coffee and with his left hand he reached out greedily for the beans that fell out.

---

[125]Frederick the Great is known in Germany by the nickname *"Der Alte Fritz,"* literally "The Old Fritz."

The Old Fritz yelled out: "Hang this thing low, so the people do not have to break their necks to look at it!"

His words were answered with tremendous laughter. The placard was torn into a thousand pieces. The King rode off, accompanied by the loud cheering of his Berliners.

A Retort

The favorite butcher of Old Fritz, who had faithfully served him for many years, was given many gifts.

As one day the wagon tipped over in bad weather and he arrived to the King coated in mud from the street, he reproached Frederick with harsh words: "That can not happen! Your Majesty has to lose a battle sometimes!"

Old Fritz laughed and gave to his favorite Butcher a gold piece.

The Picture of the King

One day as Old Fritz was out riding, he ran into an old farmer's wife and passed close to her wagon. "What do you want?" asked the King cheerfully. - "Only to see the sight of my King," answered the elder. Then the King grabbed a small gold piece from his pocket, gave it to the woman, and said: "Beloved woman, on these things I am much easier to see; on there you can look at me as long as you want; now I do not have time to let you contemplate me any longer."

Frederick Wilhelm, the Soldier-King

The Wigs

When Frederick Wilhelm was still Crown Prince, he went to the anteroom of the King, his father, and found there at a blazing fireplace a number of chamberlains. All stood up and greeted the Prince reverentially with a deep bow, that the locks of their great wigs nearly touched the ground. He went toward them and spoke to the vogue fools, and the entire circle nodded in accordance.

"I am so pleased", the adolescent Prince said derisively, "that you gentlemen, are so entirely in my view. Without doubt I can hope, that you will prove that also through death." All the dignitaries levied and bowed mutely.

"Then I take the men by their word," exclaimed the Crown Prince, as he took his small simple wig from his head and flung it into the fire in the fireplace, "he is a scoundrel, who will not follow me!"

Horrified, the gentlemen looked at one another. But the glaring look of the Prince left them no choice. With hard hearts each took his gorgeous, so expensive wig and flung it into the fireplace.

Frederick Wilhelm and his Grenadiers

A young shepherd from a small municipality in Hannover sat in a bar with a foreigner. They were discussing going into the service of the Duke of Anhalt-Dessau. But he had no inclination to. He reckoned that the foreigner was a Prussian recruiter. Then, he should watch him. The war-chest in Hannover was at 50 *Thalers*, and needed a Prussian recruiter fast. Then the foreigner said, he was only a shopkeeper. A few days later the shepherd met the foreigner again, who invited him up in his wagon to get a part for his gate. They were barely outside, when three men came up the stairs and chained him at the hands and feet. Three days they drove and brought the young shepherd to Potsdam, taking the Long Chap[126] into the barracks of the Grenadiers of King Frederick Wilhelm I. The foreigner was indeed a recruiter for the King Frederick Wilhelm I of Prussia, who toured across all the lands and recruited young men with persuasion, guile, and force.

Now the new Grenadier sat there, in a blue coat with white vest, white pants and gaiters in one of the many small houses that were in the garrison in Potsdam. More than 2000 "Long Chaps" the King had here. None were under 2 meters tall. The *Flügelmann*[127]

---

[126]*Lange Kerle*: Wilhelm I created a regiment, the "Long Chaps" consisting of the tallest soldiers possible, ostensibly because it was easier for them to shoot a longer, and thus more accurate, muzzle-loading firearm.

[127]Literally "Wing Man": the soldier on the flank of a column who sets the standard of march, known in North American military parlance as a "marker."

was over 2 ¼ meters. The married men lived with their families. The unmarried men, four to a house, must take care of their own domestic situation. Their uniforms must be immaculate. The hair must be powdered, the leather fixings whitened. Only the food was simple.

On duty, when the King often led them himself, it was difficult. If a button was missing off a uniform, he would strike unrelentingly with his cane.

Nevertheless the Long Chaps loved their King. They thought of him as their father, and they his children. He was so frugal, but he would allow promotions and endowments to his long Grenadiers no matter the cost. Indeed he would not lose any of his precious famed Grenadiers. He hanged deserters. One time he was notified of a very unlucky circumstance, which caused him fear. When he heard, that the tower of St. Peter's Church in Rome had fallen, he reckoned, with fear, that the *Flügelmann* of his Grenadiers was killed.

The Grenadiers had to be well trained, in drills and steps they learned to march. They learned weapons handling with iron ramrods, so when the King's best friend the Duke of Dessau came over, they had practiced so long that with great precision and unity they could all move together. Five shots a minute was the norm. "In battle they would attack with great swiftness," reckoned the King. The soldiers were forbidden alcohol. Each was educated to be a true professional chap.

When the detail was over, the King often talked with the Grenadiers, asked about their wives and children, and became a godfather to one or another of the children.

For defiance and sloth he would order the gauntlet. The accused must run through a lane, in which 200 Grenadiers were placed. They must hit him with a cane, and often he would break down halfway through and join back with them with a bloody back.

Once the Long Chaps took the King on their hunting trip. The hunters strode through the forest, and in the evenings sat in the castle with their guests, emissaries, ministers, and councils and spoke with them over tobacco pipes.

The Costly Lunch

One time Frederick Wilhelm I walked, as he loved to do, alone through the streets of Potsdam. It was around 12 o'clock, and a housewife had just put lunch on the table, and the family had come together. The door of the house stood open, and lured by the aroma of the dish, the King walked in.

"What have you cooked there?" he said. "It smells so appetizing." - "Ah, your majesty," said the housewife, "it is an ordinary meal, like any poor worker has. Tripe with white turnips."

"I did not know that," answered the King, "but I am curious; I will eat with you!" And so he seated himself between the housemates. It was delicious to him, and it pleased him when the housewife told him it only cost two *Groschen*.[128]

On the next day, Frederick Wilhelm ordered his cook to prepare this dish one time for the royal table. He did; but when the King assessed the price of the recipe he noticed that the cook had spent 10 *Taler*[129] for the tripe with white turnips, he burst out in anger and thoroughly thrashed the deceiver with a cane.

---

[128]20 cents.
[129]10 silver coins.

Frederick Wilhelm, the Great Elector

The Greatest Victory

When Frederick Wilhelm grew up, he was sent by his parents to Holland. He wanted to learn about the nation and powerful land. His home Brandenburg suffered harshly at that time after the great battle. The table of the electors, his father's, was only rarely summoned. Also, Holland lay in battle, but the young national aristocracy, with whom he came together, ran reckless lives. They demanded the strange Prince-son out, to end their horrible tribulation. But Frederick Wilhelm rejected that: "I take on your horrible strike impartially. That I owe to my honor, my land and my parents." Still in the same night he departed with few escorts and rode to the field camp of the Prince of Orange, who just besieged the fortress at Breda. When the commander of the cause learned of his arrival, he said: "My Prince, your flight proves more valorous than when I conquered Breda. Greatness comes to he who knows how to overcome on his own."

How Stettin was Besieged

In the war against the Swedish, the Elector was besieging the city of Stettin, which was under Swedish rule. The residents of Stettin thought, however, that the Brandenburgers could not wear them down, and in order to flout the Elector, they harvested the cornfield on the outside of the city for the view of the beleaguers, that could be used as a natural cover, and took the corn around the battlements and decorated the city with it. In their over-confidence they hung on the tower of St. Mary's Church a giant one, made out of wood. From there they could see the Brandenburg Field Marshall Derfflinger, who in his youth went out in the world to be a tailor.

Then the Elector vowed: "Sooner would I go to the grave for Stettin, than return to Saxony empty-handed!"

The noose was tightening ever more on the city. For many days the blistering cannons shot on the fortress, until finally no house in Stettin was undamaged. The major assault on the city was already underway, when finally the City Council Delegation was sent to the Elector and begged for mercy. "We plead in meekness and humility," said their head speaker, "and promise that in the future we will show the Elector of Brandenburg every bit of dedication we have shown Sweden."

The answer of the Elector was gracious: "All is in the past," he said, "we should forgive and forget. I will rebuild the burned church at all costs, and also restore the city to its former strength."

And the Elector kept his word. As he made peace with the city again, and the Swedes had to step down, the damage of the siege was repaired and all was well again.

Paul Beneke, a German Naval Hero

The Foundling

At the time, when Danzig was a powerful Hanseatic city, a large Danzig cog returned one time from a far sea voyage. As she encountered the Baltic Sea of the homeland, she was caught in the night in a thick fog that obscured vision. It was too late when the captain noticed a small sailing ship. It surged suddenly toward his cog out of the mist and crossed their bow.

An impact could no longer be avoided. From the whole striking slam of the blows in the side, the strange ship capsized and sank very fast in the waves. Her crew appeared to have found their deaths, for the life boat searched to no avail for survivors.

Soon the Captain set out again, then a seaman saw a wash basket floating on the water, and therein lay a boy, who was maybe a year old. A man hoisted him on board and brought him to Danzig. There the rich merchant Beneke took pity on the foundling; he adopted him as a son and gave him the name Paul.

The German Kind

The English had such fear of Paul Beneke, that they would not even sail out on the sea. They gave a foreign sailor much money to sail. He would wage battle on their side against the Germans. The foreigner's ship was immensely huge, and navigated the sea like a floating city, bristling with guns.

When Paul Beneke heard about it, he went immediately against the enemy, and soon he spotted the massive ship of his new opponent. He neared closer to him and called over: "Give to me your cargo in good will, ship, or we will force you to!" But over these words the enemy only smiled: "Come over here with your small rowboat", they replied, "you will be worthily received!" At that, Beneke began the battle, and let the cannons fire. But his men were timid and fearful, because the enemy ship was so massive before their eyes, and they begged their captain to cancel the battle and flee to safety. This angered Beneke and he said to his crew: "My men, what should come of this? Would we rather die as German war heroes, or will the children point their fingers at us and obit: "That is they, they who were scared away by the Welsh!?"

The crew replied: "Beloved Captain, sir, we are German and we will show the Welsh!"

Then Paul Beneke gave the order to advance on the enemy ship and to assault it. Before the enemy could see it, the Germans were up next to the ship and began to storm onto it, by any means that came to mind. Soon the enemy ship was given over, and the Captain knelt before Beneke and begged for his life.

Then Beneke showed himself as a true German warrior. "Stop," he called to his people, "please be merciful to the besieged, who are humbled in grace!" - So the weapons were lowered, the enemy gave themselves up as prisoners, and Paul Beneke navigated the seized ship with all its cargo to his homeland.

Henning Schindekopf, The Marshall of the German Knighthood

A Valiant Knight

Two men rode on a dirt path through the dense forest of East Prussia. The one carried heavy iron armor and his white cloak with the black cross on it showed that he belonged to the German Knighthood. He had with him important letters that he should bring to the Grand Master of the order in Marienburg.

His companion, who rode behind him, was a simple cavalry Knight. His name was Henning Schinderkopf, and as one could notice from his accent, he was from the German North Sea coast, where his parents owned a farmstead.

The two riders made their way calmly, when they suddenly came under attack by five armed men, who sprang forth out of the darkness. "Save yourself and bring the letters in security! I will keep these fellows at bay", exclaimed Henning Schinderkopf to the Knight, as he drew is sword and lunged upon the enemy. With weighty strikes he struck two of the opponents down in succession. The third sprang at him and wounded him in his left arm; now with a split open head he also fell to the soil. Now the fourth attempted to insidiously strike Henning's horse down. But the Knight would not let the plight of his companion be marooned. He came forward to the enemy and struck him with his sword on the hand. Then both of the last opponents disappeared in the darkness of the woods.

The Knight scantily bandaged the wound of Henning Schindekopf, and then both rode to Marienburg. When the Grand Master found out what had occurred, he praised the valiance of the servant and promised to reward him for his efforts.

Kaiser Frederick Barbarossa[130]

The Chess Game

When King Konrad lay on his deathbed, he had Duke Frederick von Staufen be summoned to him, handed over to him the crown, *Reichs*-sword and scepter and ordained him as his successor.

In the night ensuing thereafter, Frederick von Staufen found no sleep. He sat alone, absorbed in thought, in his room, that was lit only by candlelight. Then suddenly the light from the candle flickered, for the door was flung open. His Uncle Otto came in, who was Bishop of Freising, and a man of high consequence. "You grasp after the crown", he said to Frederick, "but you know also, how hard and perilous your Kingship will be?" And the old man conjured up Frederick against becoming King; he had liked the young Prince as did everyone who knew him.

In order to make the Duke give up on his proposition, he asked him urgently: "Have you also considered how many enemies you stand against, if you became King?" – "Consider this here!" said Frederick. He grabbed the figures of a chess game and set the white King on the board; it should be the German King.

---

[130]In the original, *Rotbart*, literrally "Red Beard." Hitler had named his invasion of the Soviet Union in 1941 "Barbarossa," the Latin name of Frederick I, to draw a parallel between the crusades to the holy-land and the German invasion of Russia for living-space.

For each enemy that the Bishop named, he would set a black figure against him.

Then Otto named as the first the Pope, and Frederick stood the black King up. Now named was Henry the Lion, and then Staufer grabbed the next game piece, the black Queen. For the Duke of Welf[131] he set a Bishop, for the Archbishop of Mainz the other. For the rebellious cities in Italy he set the towers and the Knights on the board and for the army of the Normans all the black pawns. Then the Bishop was finished with his accounting, and there stood against the white King all the black figures. Around both of the men was the still of the night, and remaining silent they looked upon this picture of the world, wherein the German King stood alone against an overwhelming force.

In the end the Bishop asked: "Will you really play this despairing King's game?" But Frederick asked in retort: "If I do not do it, who will?"

Otto did not know how to answer, and how he now saw Staufer, young and strong, manly and beautiful, and in his countenance a holy sobriety without any arrogance – that had won him over. "You have my vote in the election", he said to Frederick, "and I will tout for you everywhere."

The *Reichs*-Festival in Mainz

---

[131] Also known as Guelph.

The young King Henry, the son of Frederick Barbarossa, had reached the age of 19 years, and thus could arise as a Knight; and the King designated that there would be an event for the Pentecost in the city of Mainz.

In the old city on the Rhine there were so many guests, they simply could not grasp the number. There the *Kaiser* had a festival city built in the square, on the Rhine, and the Main Rivers. It was entirely made out of wood, and even with all the things that were made - a King's palace, a Church, with houses for all the guests and hoards, there were still oversights. Thus there was a whole tent-city too. Two big houses were filled top to bottom with roosters and hens, up and down the Rhine came the wine ships loaded with large barrels of wine.

From all points on the compass people came here, the Dukes, Margraves, Palatinate Dukes, and landed Noblemen, the *Reich*'s Knights and elders, and the Archbishops and Bishops and Abbots. And one could find others in their entourages who came; the Duke of Bohemia came with 2000 men, from Austria 5000, and Bernhard of Saxony came with a massive 7000 men. And it was not only their numbers that was meaningful, but also the expense of their garb and their choice horses. One could put the number at 40 000, and each one was the *Kaiser*'s guest for three days. And also in the masses there were various bandsmen and traveling entertainers and uncounted people.

On the day of the Pentecost the huge festival
began with a religious service. In the main procession
strode the *Kaiser* and *Kaiserin* and their son King Henry,
wearing crowns. At the feast that happens this day, the
King would serve the Dukes and Margraves.

On the next day the *Kaiser*'s son was Knighted.
His father gave him the sword and handed him the
shield and spear. All the chiefs endowed the young
Knight with gifts of steeds and expensive clothing, that
showed the wealth of the guests. Then the lord rode a
large tournament, and then the old *Kaiser* did it for all as
well.

So went many days of the joyous festival, but it
was not all tournaments and dances, feasts and
drinking. One could also hear poets and singers, whom
the *Kaiser* had brought to the festival. They sang later

and long into these days in Mainz, to show the Lordship of the *Reich* and of the *Kaiser* how wonderful the festival was.

Henry the Lion

The Lion from Braunschweig

In ancient times Duke Henry went out on adventures to distant, unknown lands in which no men lived. When he one time went through a broad, wild forest, he saw a dreadful dragon in a spat with a lion, and the lion appeared to be in desperate need. Since, however, the lion was a high animal and the dragon evil and poisonous, Henry sprang to the lion with his help. The dragon shrieked a cry that pealed through the woods for miles around and fended a long time; finally, however, the hero succeeded in killing him with his good sword. Then the lion approached him, lay down at the Duke's feet and would forsake him nevermore from this hour.

As the loyal animal fed his rescuer with captured game, the Duke built a raft out of bound wood and set it on the sea. Next he would escape out of this solitude and the company of the lion to live amongst men. When one time the lion went into the woods in order to hunt, Henry climbed onto his vessel and pushed off from the bank. The animal however, on his return found his master gone and saw him afar on the sea; he sprang instantly in the waves and swam so long, until he was on the raft by the Duke. There he lay down quietly at his feet.

Thereafter they drove long upon the sea, and soon hunger and misery overcame them. There appeared to the hero the evil devil and he spoke: "Duke, I bring to you a message! This evening an alien prince will end your marriage with your wife; seven years have elapsed already since your voyage. I will carry you to your wife today, if you will be mine!" Sadly, Henry retorted: "Your message may very well be true, yet I will trust in God, who makes all certain." Then said the devil: "God does not help you in your hardship, I, however, will carry you along with the lion from Giersberg for Braunschweig and set you there. Then you will wait for me. If I find you asleep on my return, however, then you will belong to me and my empire!"

The Duke, who became pained from burning desire after his beloved wife, took on this suggestion and hoped upon heaven's help against all the art of evil. Thus the Devil took him quickly through the air toward Braunschweig, set him down on Giersberg and exclaimed: "Now watch, I will return again!" Henry however, was so tired, and sleep overcame him. The Devil came back, in order to get the Lion, and came there soon with the loyal animal through the air.

As he saw the Duke sink in exhaustion on the mountain, he rejoiced already; but the lion, who would die for his master, started out in a roar, so that Henry instantly awoke. Then the evil enemy saw his game lost, and he threw the lion from the air to the earth so that it cracked. The animal came, luckily, up the mountain to his master, who thanked god for his rescue. Then the Duke Henry went with the lion past the mountain out of which strapped the loud noise of the commencing party. The strange guest, who knew no one else, asked for a drink of wine. And as he emptied the pitcher, he took his golden ring, threw it in, and let him bring it to the Duchess. As soon as the ring was seen, whereon the Duke's shield and name were inscribed, she turned white and ordered the stranger to make an appearance before her. Then she realized with full delight her beloved husband, called to him a wholehearted welcome, and in the great hall loud jubilation about the homecoming of the hero predominated.

Hereupon Duke Henry ruled long in his *Reich*. And as he died in old age, the lion laid upon the grave of his master and would not leave, until he too, passed away.

The animal was buried in the castle, and a memorial was built to his honor his loyalty.

Iron Teeth

After a long battle Henry the Lion had defeated the Wends[132], who lived in today's Mecklenburg. Now the whole of Wend-land, devastated and deserted, was to be compensated by being populated with new men.

---

[132]Another name for Slavs.

The Duke called for German farmers to come from the *Reich*, and they came in great numbers.

"We are going to the East land," they sang. The wooden carts jarred and groaned and ground paths in the heath land. They carried a heavy load: the iron plowshare, colliding with sacks full of state goods, hard grinding stones, textile looms, and all the accompanying household goods. These wagons always went over to the market at Braunschweig, where the settlers could get supplies at the Duke's expense before they went over the Elbe.

But the Duke was also considerate of something else. In the case of his Western Saxon lands, where there was ore in the earth, there was a family of blacksmiths. They came with them voluntarily and set out with their workshop. And to each column of farmers he gave a blacksmith on the way. They would supply the settlers with all the implements, with plows, scythes, and harrows. "We must show the Wends iron teeth," he said "or else they will beat us with wooden clubs." He knew the plowshare, harrow, and scythe were as important as weapons.

Kaiser Otto the Great

The Frankfurter Yule

Otto was born when his father was but First Duke of Saxony. His younger Brother Henry was born afterwards, when the father had then become German King. That meant Henry must actually become King after his father and not Otto, the "Son of a Duke." Against this view he was strengthened, even by his mother, who wanted to see her favorite son preferably as King - the independent and energetic Otto. Henry found many flatterers and friends among the Dukes and all of them, the lovers of a King-to-be, were free to do what they wanted. But the conjurors dashed from Otto's army, Henry fled to Saxony in the town of Merseburg. For two months Otto beleaguered the town. Then they surrendered Henry following a stalemate of 30 days, but he did not subordinate himself.

It looked bad for the German *Reich*. Henry had gone to Lorraine and launched a new insurrection.

For the third time in this year Otto had to cross over the Rhine. All the land around the Rhine was in revolt against Otto. Many were lost because they did not think that Otto should remain King.

There succeeded two Counts for the *Führer* of the rebels to attack, as they turned home from a raid and wanted to set over the Rhine. Two Dukes, leaders of the revolt, came there. Henry fled to King Ludwig of France. With him he fell as an enemy again in Germany. Otto was victorious in the struggle. Henry subjected himself to him, and Otto forgave him at the request of his Mother.

But Henry did not mean it honestly. He planned new mischief. Anywhere where unrest against King Otto lived, Henry would help stir it up. In all conspiracies he took part. When Easter came in Quedlinburg the conspirator would murder Otto and Henry would don the crown.

Otto discovered it all and knew beforehand. Sanctimoniously Henry with his attaché took part in the festival. All looked as if it was going according to the plan of conspiracy. Then as a little of the festival had passed, Otto had the killer arrested and executed before they could carry out their plan. Only Henry could escape. However he found nowhere to flee. Again Mother asked for mercy for him. Otto had him jailed in the palace in Ingelheim.

Over a year elapsed. Otto celebrated that Christmas in the Cathedral at *Frankfurt am Main*. As Otto went to early mass, Henry prostrated himself in ragged clothing and bare feet before him. Betrayal upon betrayal he had brought to bear on his Kingly brother. Otto had already forgiven him one time, and Henry was quick to plan his murder afterwards. But Otto thought of the request of his mother. And should he remain bitter now at the Festival of Peace? This time the sorrow Henry experiences is honest. The King sees this too.

The guilt confessing of the brother moved Otto. He pulled his brother up to him. With his King's jacket he shielded him against the cold.

Since this day Henry was the truest help to his brother in the struggle for the unity and greatness of the *Reich*.

Hermann Billung

In the time that King Otto ruled over Germany, he rode once with a heavily harmed group of horsemen together through the Lunenburg Heath. Somewhere off the trail a fourteen year old boy minded the herd of his father; and when he saw the warriors were coming by and noticed their gleaming helmets and harnesses, he said to them: "How magnificent that looks! If only I could be such a proud horseman!"

Then the convoy arched off the road and came cross-country to the spot where the boy was minding the flock.

That was, however, bad; this field belonged to his father. He went there and opposed the horsemen, stood in their way, and yelled with a bold tone: "Turn back! The streets are yours, the field is mine!" From the head of the convoy rode a man with a high form and a lordly look. He looked in wonder at the boy who dared to get in their way. But he took pleasure in the fortunate youth, who stood up to them with courage and fearlessness and did not yield his spot.

"Who are you, boy?" he asked.

"I am Hermann Billung's eldest son and my name is also Hermann. You may not ride over my father's field!"

"I will anyhow," demanded the Knight, "and I suggest you back down!"

The boy then looked with burning eyes at the Knight and spoke without stepping down: "Law must remain law! You do not have permission to ride over this field without riding over me on the way!"

Then the Knight responded threateningly: "Is it right if you refuse to obey your King? I am Otto, your King!"

"No, you are not King Otto, of whom I have heard so much from my father," retorted Hermann

Billung; "King Otto protects the law, and you break the law. King Otto does not do that, says my father!"

"Take me to your father, brave boy!" said the King, and his earnest look turned completely joyful and mild.

"There is my father's home," answered Hermann, "but I can not take you there, as I cannot lose the herd. If you are really King Otto, go back to the street, as the King protects the law."

King Otto complied and rode back onto the street. To the father of the boy he said: "Let me take your son with me! He is a loyal man, and I need loyal men."

Hermann Billung grew into a valiant hero in a royal home. Otto treated him as a true friend, and made him an honorary Duke of the *Reich* on the lower Elbe. Hermann guarded and minded his domain so loyally, as he had once done on his father's property.

King Henry

How Henry Became King

King Konrad had been badly wounded in battle. As he felt his end was near, he called his brother Eberhard to him and said to him: "Beloved brother, I feel I will soon die. Hear my words and follow my council! We can muster and lead the army, we have fortresses and weapons and everything that it takes for Kingly dignity. To us has come proficiency and luck. Both things, as well, has Duke Henry of Saxony, and in his hands alone lays the salvation of the *Reich*. Now take the symbols of Kingly dignity, the holy lance, the golden sheath by the fireplace, the sword and the crown of old Kings. Bring them to the Duke of Saxony and make peace with him! He has become a King in wartime and ruler of many people!" - Eberhard told all to do what his brother had asked of him. After Konrad's death he brought himself to Saxony and handed over to the Duke Henry, as the new King, the symbols of his high office.

In Fritzlar Eberhard assembled the leaders and the elders of Saxony and Franconia and proclaimed for all people Duke Henry as King. And the assembly celebrated the new sovereign and greeted him as their lord. Now the leader of Bishops came forward and set the crown on the chosen, and anointed him with holy oil, then he stepped back and King Henry said: "Through the grace of God and through the choice of the people I am King. That is enough for me. Anointing and crowning are but a worthy bestowing. Of such an honor I am not yet worthy." After these words loud applause filled the room. The Bishop made the sign of the anointment to signify the supreme rule of the Pope over the King. The King would later strain such a challenge to his independence from the Church. All hoisted their righteous emperor and celebrated again: "Hail King Henry!"

Duke Arnulf of Bavaria would not subject himself to the new King or pledge obedience to him. The King went there with an army to oppose the Duke in the field and beleaguered him in Regensburg. Before he showed the power of his army in battle, however, King Henry requested cleverly to meet the Duke alone. Arnulf thought, after old customs, a duel of both leaders should be done. He appeared in the agreed location armed. Henry, however, came without weapons, so that he might make good again with the Duke. - As Arnulf stood before him, the King spoke majestically: "The people have chosen me as King by God's will, and it is a rebellious stance, if you yourself go against God's command. Had the people destined you to be the King, I would yield to you without hesitation." These words went straight to the heart of Arnulf. He deliberated with his council, and then submitted himself to King Henry and recognized him as his lord. - So King Henry led the *Reich*, without spilling German blood in battle.

The Clash in Hungary

In the time when King Henry reigned, the Hungarians were pouring into Germany, and their wild troops of horsemen laid waste far and wide. Cities, towns, and villages were burned down. On small fast horses they rode with the wind. They shot their arrows at their opponents while riding. They horribly murdered all men and made off with women and children. King Henry made war with them but not enough to expel the enemy permanently from the land. It was so serious for the Saxons, that they were driven far from their homes. They could not help any others, and there were no cities that they could flee to.

One day a warrior of Henry's made a good catch. He assailed a house of the enemy's, took their chief, a Prince of Hungary, prisoner and brought him to King Henry. Soon thereafter an envoy from Hungary arrived, and as they were taken before the King, they said: "Set our Prince free, we will pay you a great reward!" But King Henry answered: "I will not accept your treasure, but I will set the prisoner free, if you keep out of my lands for nine years." The Hungarians agreed to that; they stipulated however, that and the end of each year, he pay them a tribute, and Henry agreed to that willingly.

Henry used the year of the cease-fire to prepare his Saxons to go to war with the Hungarians. Each farmer had to retain a horse to ride and go to war with. The farmers were trained in units by their Lords. They were armed with shields and lances. They had to learn to fight with a sword from the back of a horse. In a battle against the Slavs they tested the war-readiness of their army. The Wends had retreated to their swamp fortress. But Henry gave chase. As the bog cooled, they went over the ice with their troops and took the fortress island Brandenburg. Then they went through the territory to the city Meißen until they reached Prague. There they pressured the Bohemian King to submit. He set his new cavalry troop on and trained them to battle with the great enemy, the Hungarians.

In the country he built castles. The many cities, like Merseburg, had to secure themselves with stone masonry, the towns and villages had to set up ditches and walls. In the whole land there was so much work and preparation done for the inevitable battle. By Goslar he built the great castle Werla. From the warriors, who must live off the land, every ninth must make living quarters in the city for himself and the others. The other eight must sow, harvest, and bring the yield.

As the ninth year was upon them, the envoy came to collect their tribute. There he laid a mangy dog, that someone had killed, at the foot of the Hungarian: "That should be your tribute!" he yelled out. "If you want something else, all of you can come here. You will find us ready!"

The tenth year after the cease-fire came upon them. King Henry was terribly ill, as the Hungarian messenger approached him. Likewise he sent his messenger across all of Saxony and told all warriors to come to him as soon and as quickly as possible. And soon, after four days, he had assembled a large Army group, that there was no Saxon fit for military service who was not there. - And even though the King was sick and faint, he mounted his horse, called his men to him, and spoke to them: "We Saxons will not bend our necks for the Hungarians; indeed, we will show them that we know how to wield our swords. If the battle begins, none of the others rush ahead, also if one has a fast horse, stay united with your shields until the first arrow of the Hungarians flies toward us. Then storm against the enemy with all your might and rout him with your swords before he has the chance to launch a second arrow!" The Hungarians came in powerful droves. They came in many swarms that moved West. One was struck from the Saxon and Thuringian cavalry. As the other Hungarians drove upon them, they sounded the signal to fire. Their smoke called the swarms to a rally. But soon Henry moved up. The army flew the royal flag. Now Henry tried to fool the Hungarians. He let his Thuringian foot soldiers go out and draw the Hungarian cavalry army in. The Hungarians drove upon the foot soldiers. Then they

were in their grips the ready Saxon cavalry were sent
on.

"Kyrie eleison,"[133] or in German "Lord, have
mercy on us!" was the war-cry of the Saxons, when the
Hungarians burst out with their devilish roaring cry.[134]
So, just as the King had said, they drew together with
their shields and blocked the arrows of the enemy
without trouble. Then they rushed the enemy with a
rapid approach and eliminated the Hungarians. Then
the enemy soon turned away and retreated from battle.
They jettisoned their bows and arrows and costly
weapons on the way, and also got rid of their harnesses,
so their horses could run unhindered.

So the Hungarians were partly slaughtered and
had partly escaped, and the countless prisoners, who
they made off with, were returned to freedom. Most of
the Hungarians who were freed only barely made it.
But soon the *Reich* was no longer a wasteland. The
army, that the King had forged, had stood as strong as
the stone walls in the cities and towns.

---

[133]Transliterated from the Greek.
[134]*Hui-Hui-Geschrei.*

Kaiser Charlemagne[135]

The Iron Karl[136]

The Germanic peoples had spread out all over Europe and lived in many isolated towns and Kingdoms. Then Karl, the King of the Franks, undertook the task of uniting all Germanic people in a vast Germanic empire and diminishing the occupying Slavs in the old Germanic lands in the East. Thus he also thought he must win the Germanic people who lived in Italy and in Spain for his *Reich*.

With a mighty army he undertook an expedition over the Alps against the Langobard King Desiderius. He fled, however, inside his fortress city when he heard of the arrival of the great Frankish army.

When Karl came after him, Desiderius went up a high tower with a Frankish Count named Otker so they could look out over the land. First he saw the formations of the Frankish army, and Desiderius spoke: "Is Karl perhaps in this great army?" Then Otker, who had lived in Karl's home for a long time, gave the answer: "Not yet!" Then came the army of many peoples, assembled from across the *Reich*, and Desiderius turned again to Okter: "Is Karl likely under these warriors?" Otker again answered: "Not right yet."

---

[135]The German name for Charlemagne is *Karl der Große*, literally "Charles the Great" but the former is substituted for the familiarity of the English reader.
[136]Charles, left in its original German spelling.

- He began to quiver and shake and said: "I do not know what we should do then, if Karl intends to go against us with such a group of warriors."

Then the Bishop appeared, the Abbot, and other spirituals with their attendants and stammeringly brought the word to Desiderius: "Let us descend and hide underground against the wrath of such a terrible enemy!" Otker, who had learned all about Karl's war armaments, said: "That is not Karl yet. At first you must see the iron stare and the iron will flooding the fortress walls, then you can expect Karl."

No sooner had his speech ended, as a cloud appeared from the West. It was the Franks and with them Iron Karl, dressed in his iron helmet and wearing iron armor, a plate on the chest and both shoulders. In his left hand he held a beautiful iron lance, and in the right hand, always at the ready, the undefeated sword which was used to lead. His limbs were covered with iron scales; not only was his shield iron, but his steed was also armored with iron. Onward and unrelenting came the armor. Iron filled the streets and fields, it beamed like the light of the sun in their gaze. And Okter turned to Desiderius and said: "See, that is Karl, for whom you have searched all this time!" With these words the King collapsed lifeless to the ground. Soon after the Langobard nation of the Frankish *Reich* was incorporated, and Karl became King also of the Langobards. The Romans and the Pope in Rome asked Karl for help. In the year 800 Karl went to Rome. There he was crowned as *Kaiser*, so that also the Romans and the Roman Church could be seen as within his supreme Lordship.

Kaiser Karl's Grave

Kaiser Karl had waged many battles until he had secured a vast *Reich*. His name was respected and feared across the whole world. Kings of far away lands submitted themselves voluntarily to him; he was sent gifts by Arab Princes from the Orient reveling him as a powerful ruler of the world.

Many days before *Kaiser* Karl died, there was an earthquake. It was interpreted by men as a sign of the nearing death of their powerful *Kaiser*. Later, one recounted, until his death the heavens became dark and gloomy, the sun and moon had darkened. The Slavs, however, who had been accepted again in all Germanic lands, and who had fought his power, miscalled their most powerful prince Křl, that is "Karl," after his name, as the most important to reign of all time.

When *Kaiser* Karl died, he was interred in a new tomb worthy of his greatness, on a throne of marble sitting upright, on his brow the crown and in his hand the scepter, and in the other the *Evangelienbuch*,[137] then the tomb was closed over him and sealed off with stone. That took place on the second day after the death of the

---

[137]A poetic religious tome written by German Monk Otfrid of Weissenburg circa 871.

great ruler, and no man saw him again, until the year 1000.

Kaiser Otto III of the Saxon tribe coveted the *Reichs* crown. He wanted to see the corpse of *Kaiser* Karl. He went to the grave, led by two Bishops and a Count, and had an opening made into the tomb. There sat high and tall, like a stone monument on his marble throne, the buried *Kaiser*, even after the passage of two hundred years, the crown on his brow, the scepter in his hand and the book on his knee. All the men were taken aback in awe of the great deceased. Then *Kaiser* Otto had the grave closed and sealed off once again.

In the night afterword Karl appeared to *Kaiser* Otto in a dream, sublime and formidably real, and said to him: "Must you come and disturb my rest? Soon you will rest, where I rest, not far from me!" Otto, the *Kaiser*, took this to heart, and not many years later, still in his youth, he went to his grave in Aachen.

The Legitimate History of Lies

Widukind, Duke of the Saxons

Widukind

When Widukind was a child, he played one time on the banks of a stream. A traveler came by and told him that a leader of the Saxons had betrayed his people and had fled to the land of the Franks.

Then Widukind took the loamy sand that he found on the bank, formed it into the shape of a man, and wrote on his forehead with a pointy stone the word "Traitor." Then he grabbed his spear and thrust it angrily into the man, until he was entirely obliterated. Then he proclaimed for all time: "So it should always go for one who becomes a traitor to his people!"

Only when Widukind was a Duke and he could now put an end to Saxon autonomy, did the King of the Franks come to him.

As Duke Widukind must yield to King Karl[138], he conspired with many of his confidants in his castle. He could not get his persecutor, because his horse's shoes were put on wrong. If the trails in the country were dried up, and he was home, and if he took the hill that lead to the castle, he would fly through the countryside on his fast steed and gather his supporters for a new battle.

---

[138] Charlemagne

Since only Widukind lived in his castle at the time, King Karl would betray him. He dispatched his warriors to catch the Duke. Widukind, however, was warned just in time; he mounted his most loyal steed and fled from the Frankish warriors. They set on after him, however, and there was so many of them that they found him fast. Widukind could hear the snorting of their steeds, so close was he to the heels of the enemy. That was the way that the Duke had stalked them, and came to a closed barricade. His stallion stopped and would not jump over it, the persecutors were soon near. In his need Widukind pleaded:

> "Stallion, spring tall,
> Fight the high wall.
> If you do not spring tall,
> You and I both shall fall."[139]

That encouraged the wise animal and it shot like an arrow over the barrier. The Franks, however, did not succeed at jumping the barrier and Widukind was saved.

Eventually, however, King Karl brought the Saxon Duke Widukind under his power. He regarded his prisoner in high honor and had him eat with him daily at his table.

---

[139]This poem has been very liberally translated: *"Hengstken, spring awer, Kriegst 'n Spint Hawer. Springst du night awer, fräten di un mi die Rawer."*

When the King with his high council had settled down for a meal, it was expected of him to take the seat of honor at the end of the table. He had a poor person sit there, however, so that they could eat their portion in comfort; now they had to sit on the floor. The captive Duke Widukind noticed, and as he sat down for mealtime one day, he said to the King: "Our Christian God said: 'The poor should be treated as you would treat me.' With what right do you insist that we Saxons stick our necks out for your Christian God when you handle him so contemptibly?" - The King was struck in the heart and moved by these words, because the Christian teachings struck him so from the mouth of a pagan. From then on he let the poor person bring a table and stool and have his meal right there. Widukind was set free soon thereafter with his help.

Widukind's Last Day

Duke Widukind loved birds. He found an intimate spot in an alder copse, where he liked to think; there he laid a bird trap and built a birdhouse. He had two attendants here, to care for the birds.

His most beloved spot however was a tall ash, one place, where one could see far and wide across the fertile hill country. There was there an ancient oak as well. Here he made a lookout tower that looked far out into the land, for which he had so long fought and his power had stretched out over. And the residents came and shooed away his worries and brightened his dim hours; then he did not forget, how many hard times his people had endured.

Once a rumor was started that the Duke had died. There was great sorrow in the land, and his loyal followers rushed to him to give him his last service. He was baffled as they all came into his house; and as he heard what the reason was, he smiled and said he would be thankful for it.

Unrest was brewing in the East, however, and he could not remain in his castle. In the evening he had his white horse saddled and rode off in the darkness through the land. He was gone for some time, and when the Saxons heard him in the night, they would say: "That is our Duke, he quests for the old Gods!" And they indeed thought that Wode,[140] the God of Gods, rode through the land, and they hid themselves in their houses. -

---

[140]One of the most widely known of the ancient Anglo-Saxon pagan gods.

When Duke Widukind felt that it was time for him to die, he called all of his followers together and rode with them to a castle. Out of all the huts the Saxons came and looked on at the strange column. As they saw their Duke, it frightened them, as they thought that he was coming for them now. Widukind had all the horns play once more, and it echoed through the night and all hearts trembled as they now went to their last victorious battle against the enemy. Then they left the castle, and the Duke rode off with all of his loyal followers. There was no man who stayed behind. The castle was closed up again. The people then said: "Now he is going to Wode and remains always on guard."

Arminius, the Liberator of the Germanians

Arminius and Segestes

For a long time the Romans would conquer and rule what the Germanians called Germany. They came with their large army and subjected many tribes of Germanians and forced them into servitude. Their cruel pursuit would bring on the drive for freedom.

One evening Varus, the commander of the Romans, sat with a few officers of his army in his tent for a meal. Also Arminius, a Count of the Cherusci tribe, and his Uncle[141] Segestes were going. There, Varus turned to Arminius and said: "What I hear, is that a Germanic tribe is resisting Roman army service. I will go there with my army and quash the riot. But with this I need the help of your troops. When can your people be ready to march out?"

"They are good!" answered Arminius.

Segestes heard these words. He knew for a long time, how much Arminius hated the Roman oppressors. He had always secretly informed Varus for the Cherusci prince. Now he sprang up and with a sharp tone between them. "You say they are good? How is that good? For what goal are you going to assemble an army other than to rule the land in freedom?" At best, Arminius would thrust his sword through a traitor.

---

[141] Actually Arminius' father-in-law.

Should all true effort and hope to bring his people to freedom be ruined now by this traitor? Therefore he handled it quickly and replied calmly: "I have asked all of the princes to come to a caucus. No Germanic Prince will come to a caucus without bringing many warriors with him. That is all I can tell you."

Then Segestes said to the chief of the Romans: "Varus, guard yourself against Arminius! He will expel the Romans from the land and has conspired to this end. I am your friend, and I tell you, to put Arminius in chains. Only then will your attack be safeguarded."

"You hate me, Segestes", interjected Arminius, "but I have no prejudice. I would give you no such trouble, to make waves between myself and Varus! It is you that has the unresolved issue." -

But Segestes came on even stronger to Varus: "I swear to you. If you do not give me credit, take both Arminius and myself prisoners and wait to see who is right, he or I!" -

Varus smiled and said: "I think more of Arminius than you. From him I have nothing to fear."

Arminius, the Liberator

It was the day after this meeting between Arminius, Segestes, and Varus. The Roman army was taken to the summer camp of Varus. Arminius was instructed by Varus to muster his Germanic warriors and put down a rebellion with the Romans. Likely the army of Varus was on any day about 25 000 men strong. Carelessly the troops marched there. Majestic sunlight lay over the opposition, through which they passed. Joyfully the Trumpets burst on the pinnacle of the columns, and the troops sang happy marching songs and joked and smiled among each other as if they went to a parade, not to a bloody battle. Varus himself rode in the midst of the columns and was joyful and in good spirits. He vaunted himself, how he had cut short the rebellion and put it down, and then indeed had defeated the other chiefs in most severe circumstances.

Gradually, however, a change came on in the territory where the army was. Heavy rains poured down, and howling gusts of the storm came down on the heights. Soon the trails were slippery, and with each step the heavily armored soldiers sank deeper into the muck on the trails. The march went now through endless forests. The soil was boggy, and in places wide ditches filled with water and dense undergrowth slowed the progress of the columns. The forward detachment must bridge and go over the waterlogged trail and with their hatchets clear a path through the undergrowth of the forest. After this following them a wagon was hauled across with the others in it. Soon there came a general muddle. For a long time the joyful tunes of the trumpets were silenced, and the happy songs of the men were replaced by curses and insults over the Germanic people, their unwelcoming forests, and their unkempt trails.

Then suddenly came a loud alarm call from the back of the columns. Arrows were flying out of the bushes.

"To the weapons! Enemy! Enemy!" was the cry as the row broke out. Hold on - the enemy, where was he? One determined warrior sprung from the trail into the thicket, to fight the enemy, but he saw nothing. The shooters had instantly disappeared, as soon as they saw the pursuer, and soon thereafter a new salvo of arrows flew in the rows of Romans, and even louder went the call: "Enemy, Enemy!" There was a strict command given to the columns. They moved in close to each other, with all the troops together, and in all-around defense moved, with the non-combatants in the middle, and marched out again as an army column. But as the evening came nearer and nearer, and the support personnel could not come to an agreement as to where the army should arrive, they took to Varus the dire notion, that Segestes on the previous evening had spoken. Now he had only one wish: that he could bivouac as well as possible with his troops. Soon darkness fell upon them, as they reached an open area in the middle of the forest, that they found suitable. In the best order the bivouac was erected with walls and ditches and with double posts all around. Soon in the middle they started a massive bonfire. Varus had as much of his supply of fuel as could be brought from the rear, burnt. In a battle meeting it was decided to march out of the area of resistance as fast as possible and of all things they needed to do, to reach the fortress of Castle Aliso. The night went quietly.

The horn blared early the next morning in the Roman camp. The army assembled under their glorious war flag. Varus kept in mind to use the favorable nature of the locality and bring the fight to the Germanians. In defensive battle order his troop moved on, but the enemy did not show himself again. Arminius knew the superiority of the Romans in open field battles, therefore he had forbidden all of his men to go against the enemy in the open. Varus waited in vain for an attack, then went in the direction of Aliso.

The army was only barely moving into the narrow mountain valley when the Germanians showed themselves again, but more bold and open than on the day before. They no longer battled from a distance with arrows out of their hiding places. Now they stormed them with brandished lances, then the soldiers exchanged the lances for sword fight after sword fight. Many Romans fell on this day of the fight. Varus' Legion was indeed almost melted together, as he for the second time built a bivouac. Only with their last strength could the tired troops erect walls and dig trenches, then they sank exhausted to the forest floor.

It was barely the next morning when the rest of the Roman troops was broken as the battle renewed, and harder than before, it began. The Romans now stood against Arminius with his Cheruscian men. The forest valley was somewhat wider, so that the

Germanics could go against the armored Romans on foot.

Arminius had ordered a broad, final attack on the hated Romans and fought himself in the forward-most column. The long unrelenting fury against the oppressors of the Germanic people came with a terrible outburst. The Romans fell in rows, and those who scattered to find their salvation in flight were caught up with and fell in one-on-one combat. Varus would not live through the stigma of defeat and killed himself with his sword. Only a small pile of Romans, came out with their wives and children, who were going along with the support column. The news of the victory of Arminius awakened in the Germanians a great pride; the Romans however, were frightened. Through this victory Arminius secured the freedom of the Germanians. And if the Romans had sometime tried to cross over the Rhine, they would have to suffer through the victory of Arminius and his fame and eminence, and so they never again tried to undermine the pride of the Germanians.

Addendum 1 - List of the Series

The *Volk und Reich* series consisted of seven volumes and is provided here for reference. This translation is Class 1 and the only volume available in English.

Klasse 1, Von Fuhrern und Helden, Erzahlung der deutschen geschichte. (This volume) Course 1, Of Leaders and Heroes, Tales of German History.

Klasse 2, Indogermanen und Germanen. Course 2, Indogermanics and Germanics

Klasse 3, Das Erste Deutsche Reich (von 919 bis 1648). Course 3, The First German *Reich* (from 919 until 1648).

Klasse 4, Preußen und Deutschland (von 1648 bis 1871). Course 4, Prussia and Germany (from 1648 until 1871).

Klasse 5, Von der Wiederaufrichtung des Reiches durch Bismarck bis zur Gegenwart. Course 5, From the Resurrection of the *Reich* through Bismarck to the Present.

Klasse 6, Von der Urzeit bis zum Ende der Hohenstaufen. Course 6, From Primitive Times to the End of the Swabian Dynasty.

Klasse 7, Von der Deutschen Ostsiedlung bis zu den Anfangen Bismarcks. Course 7, From the German Settlement of the East to the Coming of Bismarck.